Deliverance:

The Missing Link To Sanctification

D1712006

Keys To Supernatural Freedom

Deliverance:

The Missing Link To Sanctification

Keys To Supernatural Freedom

by
Lee Audry Williams

Deliverance:
The Missing Link To Sanctification
Keys To Supernatural Freedom

The Scriptures used throughout this book are quoted from the *Authorized* or *New King James Version* unless otherwise noted. Bible references are taken from *Strong's Exhaustive Concordance of the Bible.* All explanatory insertions within a Scripture verse are enclosed in brackets. All non-English words are printed with English letters and italicized. All names used are fictitious and any resemblance is unintentional. The opinions and beliefs expressed in this book are not necessarily those endorsed by Heritage Ink Publishers.

Copyright ©2004 by Lee Audry Williams. All rights reserved. No part of this book may be reproduced in any form or by any electronic or mechanical means including information storage and retrieval systems without permission in writing from Lee Audry Williams, except by a reviewer, who may quote brief passages in a review.

ISBN 0-9743339-2-1

Published 2005
Printed in the United States of America

Published by

 **HERITAGE INK**

Marianna, Florida 32446
www.heritageink.com

Dedication

I dedicate this work to the memory of my beloved wife, Marilyn Williams, who sacrificed much time and prayer to my success. I am forever grateful for her encouragement and love.

Acknowledgements

First, I give all my thanks to the Holy Spirit who actually authored this book by encouraging me to write despite difficult periods of doubt and discouragement. Lord, I pray that this finished product is pleasing to you.

I want to acknowledge all of my children, Lee, Troy, Kevin and Malaika, for their love and support. I'm so proud of your continued growth and spiritual development. May you continue to do major damage against the kingdom of darkness. I really love you!

I extend a special thanks to Jean Mehi for her willingness and sacrificial time organizing and typing the initial draft.

I am sincerely grateful to Barbara Motley, for fervently standing in the gap for me as a watchman, keeping her eyes open and faithfully walking with me on different legs of my journey.

I want to give much thanks to my editor, Renita Dorsey, who worked tirelessly offering heartfelt suggestions while editing and proofing the final draft before its publication. I could not have completed this without her.

Last but not least, I am grateful for all of the intercessors and students who encouraged me with their love and contributions. May the Lord bestow tremendous blessings upon you all.

To contact Lee Audry Williams for speaking engagements
and training seminars, contact:

Merciful Ministries of Jesus Christ
P.O. Box 74494
Romulus, MI 48174-3822

www.mercifulministries.org

(734) 941-7074

Contents

Deliverance:
The Missing Link To Sanctification

INTRODUCTION

The word *sanctify* is used about forty-six times in the Old Testament and six times in the New Testament. I believe it is a very important word since it is used so many times by the Holy Spirit. It is also a word that is greatly misunderstood in the Body of Christ.

Some people believe that sanctified refers to someone who is extremely religious. The statement, "He or she is sanctified", is used to mean the person was somehow very holy, peculiar or set apart from the rest of the Body of Christ. I agree that the word sanctification does mean "to be set apart", but not necessarily from the rest of God's people; rather to be separated unto God for the work of the ministry and to actually live a life of holiness.

Sanctification is also a process that God uses to prepare us to carry more of His presence and glory. The Word of God tells us to sanctify ourselves, and "to present our bodies to God a living sacrifice, holy and acceptable unto God which is our reasonable service" (Romans 12:1). This means to sacrifice our own selfish desires and yield our bodies to God for service. 1 Thessalonians 4:3-4 tells us, **"For this is the will of God, your sanctification, that you should abstain from sexual immorality, that each of you should know how to possess his own vessel in sanctification and honor."** This Scripture speaks to us about the responsibility of setting ourselves apart from sexual immorality in order to be totally dedicated unto God. This means that **we must use our own will** to control our desires, thoughts and bodies in a manner that not only pleases God but also honors Him.

Deliverance: The Missing Link To Sanctification

In 1 Thessalonians 5:23, Paul prays that God Himself would sanctify us: "Now may the God of peace Himself sanctify you completely, and may your **whole spirit, soul, and body** be preserved blameless at the coming of our Lord Jesus Christ."

This Scripture alludes to the fact that by our willingness to obey God and act on His Word, He will complete and maintain our sanctification by His Spirit. In other words, after we have done all we can through repentance, abstinence, obedience and faith, the Holy Spirit will keep us and sustain us in a progressive state of holiness. All of this is a process: continually presenting our bodies a living sacrifice, reasonably serving Him; abstaining from sexual immorality; possessing and repossessing our vessels in honor, and allowing God to progressively complete the process; and finally, presenting us holy to Himself.

We cannot totally accomplish this sanctification without being set free from the power of Satan. Not only must our minds be changed by the Word of God, but our bodies must be made available to God for His use. As much as we may want to freely present our bodies to God, it cannot be if we are not free from the evil influence of demonic spirits. Satan not only invades our thought life, but will also inhabit our bodies. In doing so, he causes physical and mental illness that hinders us from totally surrendering to God's service.

This book is written with the intent of not only exposing Satan's work, but to reveal to you how to *possess* your vessel in honor. Through the different testimonies and circumstances, I hope to enlighten pastors, deliverance workers and intercessors about various practical methods used to administer deliverance. My intentions are to make it easy for any believer to activate the power of God to *set the captives free.*

The chapter, *Realms of Authority for Deliverance* is designed to show the conditions under which God will drive demons *out* of someone.

Introduction

As you will see, *Breaking Soul Ties and Releasing Inner Healing,* reveals how to break free of bondage and receive emotional healing. *Understanding Curses, Healing of Demonic Sicknesses,* and *Transference of Spirits* provide revelation that exposes how demons insidiously deceive, defile and oppress people and how to set them free.

Each testimony is written to inspire every reader to realize that God uses ordinary people to perform extraordinary feats. He will use anyone who is willing to not only sanctify himself, but also help someone else walk in the freedom God gave us through Jesus Christ our Lord.

Deliverance: The Missing Link To Sanctification

CHAPTER ONE

What is Deliverance?

Deliverance is setting the captives free from mental, spiritual and physical bondage (Luke 4:18). It is literally casting evil spirits out of a person's body by the power of the Holy Spirit, in Jesus' name.

Psalms 91:3 says, "Surely He shall deliver you from the snare of the fowler and from the noisome pestilence." The Hebrew word for *deliver* is *natsal*, which means *to snatch something or someone away from a captor, to defend a friend and strip him away from the enemy*.

In Luke 4:18, the word *deliverance* has a little different meaning than the above passage. It not only involves snatching someone away from the enemy, but also restoring that which was stolen by the enemy. Jesus stated – "The Spirit of the Lord is upon Me, because He has anointed Me to **preach** the gospel to the poor; He has sent Me to **heal** the broken hearted; to proclaim **liberty** to the captives and **recovery** of sight to the blind; to set at **liberty** (free) those who are oppressed (bound); to **proclaim** the acceptable year (grace, favor, ability) of the Lord."

Deliverance in this passage is the Greek word *aphesis*, which means *freedom, pardon, forgiveness, liberty, and remission of sins*. In essence, Jesus was saying, "I have come to set you free from spiritual ignorance, mental and emotional bondage, to cast out devils so you can freely perceive, receive, and serve Me."

Deliverance is pardon, forgiveness and remission of sins through the blood of Jesus. It is being set free from spiritual blindness, mental torment and demonic oppression.

The Purpose of Deliverance

One of the purposes of deliverance is to free people's bodies from sickness so that they can function normally, without encumbrances. It is freeing their minds from mental torment such as fear, anger, bitterness, rejection, and so on, so they can think like Christ and experience His perpetual peace.

The whole purpose of deliverance is to allow a person to express Christ in His fullness. It is freeing up the fruit of the Spirit (the character of Jesus) and allowing the gifts of the Holy Spirit to manifest more completely in the lives of God's people. Deliverance also brings healing to the physical body, and most of all, frees one up to experience God's love without interference.

What Are Demons?

Webster's dictionary defines the word *demon* as, *an evil spirit, a devil, a wicked entity, a disembodied spirit, a fallen angel, or a satanic spirit (of or from Satan).*

♦ **They are intelligent (they think and plan)**
(Matthew 12:44) ⁴⁴ "Then he says, 'I will return to my house from which I came.' And when he comes, he finds it empty, swept, and put in order. "Then he goes and takes with him seven other spirits more wicked than himself, and (Mark 5:7, 9, 12) ⁷ And he (the demon) cried out with a loud voice and said, "What have I to do with You, Jesus, Son of the Most High God? I implore You by God that You do not torment me."

⁹ Then He (Jesus) asked him, "What is your name?" And he answered, saying, "My name is Legion; for we are many."

[12] So all the demons begged Him, saying, "Send us to the swine, that we may enter them.' "

♦ **They are highly organized**

(Ephesians 6:12) [12] "For we do not wrestle against flesh and blood, but against principalities, against powers, against the rulers of the darkness of this age, against spiritual wickedness in the heavenly places." This Scripture implies that there is a hierarchy of demonic authority and powers that influence the affairs of mankind in every arena of life. This would include the affairs of government, politics, economics, and in all relationships, including the family.

Satan seeks to control the decision making process in the earth by controlling the thoughts of people all over the world. His intent is to set up his evil government in the home, the church, and governmental structures of the world.

Nature of Devils

John 10:10 says that Satan comes "to steal, kill and destroy." Their nature involves:

- Evil and wicked imaginations
- Perverted wisdom
- Rage and destruction
- No love/hatred
- Darkness

Purpose and Intent of Demons

Their purpose is to hinder, vex, oppress, torture, disillusion, discourage and control. Ultimately, they want to kill human beings, destroy the mind, steal someone's money and destroy relationships. Spiritually, they want to stunt an individual's growth in Christ (Romans 8:29), which is the development of the fruit of the Spirit (Galatians 5:22, 23).

How do they enter?

Demons enter an individual through generational curses which occur as a result of sins from forefathers in a family. They are visited upon the children of each generation through the operation of familiar spirits who seek to lead them into situations that would tempt them to sin (Exodus 34:7). These situations would be called *doors*, which are entrances for demons to freely operate.

Personal Sins

Through sins of omission and commission, a person can open up himself to demonic entrance. The sin of omission occurs when one refuses to do what God has commanded him to do. On the other hand, when one disobeys God by doing something that He commanded him not to do, then he has engaged in the sin of commission. A good example of one operating in the sin of omission is found in Matthew 18, when a particular servant was forgiven his own debt by his lord, but in turn, refused to likewise forgive his fellow servant. By refusing to forgive, he opened up himself to demons of torment, such as deceit, covetousness, anger, unforgiveness and greed.

King David committed the sin of not only covetousness, but also the sin of fornication. He coveted Uriah's wife, committed fornication with her, and in trying to cover up his sin, David conspired to have the man killed (2 Samuel 11:2-17). Consequently, the seeds of lust developed into the premeditated murder of innocent Uriah, a Hittite soldier in David's army. Not only did he open up himself to a demonic invasion of lust, but also opened a door for demons of lust, covetousness and murder to attack his sons. If we willfully sin, we also open the door for demon infiltration into our lives as well as the lives of our children.

Situations and Circumstances of Life

Demonic spirits will take advantage of any situation of weakness in human life. Any unguarded moment in a person's life, regardless of age, will be used by the devil as an opening to enter a person's body. Early childhood is the easiest time for demon infiltration: an alcoholic father who abuses his children or their mother will open the door for spirits of rejection, hurt, anger and hatred to enter the children. The same kind of spirits within the Dad can enter his children, especially a son, who might grow up to become an abusive husband or alcoholic, perpetuating the cycle of abuse in the next generation.

I once ministered deliverance to a woman who had lust demons of fornication, lesbianism and divination. She grew up in an environment of witches and warlocks. Her mother had friends who practiced witchcraft and divination openly. Because of her mother allowing these people free access to her daughter, the girl received the spirits through association. In many cases, one can trace the problems a person is having back to their childhood. The same demons that were operating in other people in his or her childhood, along with other spirits picked up along the way, can currently operate in that individual today.

Inheritance, the Lie

One of the most diabolic schemes that Satan uses is the lie that whatever affliction one's parents suffered, that person is bound to suffer the same affliction. Whether it is poverty, sickness, and so on, because of a lack of knowledge concerning the Word and the power of God available to us through the blood of Jesus, a person is prone to believe the lie: "Whatever your parents had, you can expect to have it as well." If the person believes the lie, he will open the door to an infirm spirit, a poverty spirit, suicidal spirit, and so on, and without any anointed intervention, that person will suffer the same way their parents did. In cases like this, curses must be broken while applying the truth to the lie. The truth is whatever God's Word says about us. The Word of God says, in Psalm 107:2, "Let the redeemed of the Lord say so, whom he hath redeemed from the hand of the enemy." We don't have to suffer from the same problems as our parents, because Jesus has "redeemed us from the curse of the law" (Galatians 3:13).

In my own life experiences, my brother and I bought into certain lies. We were told by our mother and others that if a black cat crossed your path, it would bring "bad luck". My younger brother so believed this lie, that anytime a black cat crossed his path, he would turn around and go in another direction. I remember once while he was driving, a black cat crossed the street in front of him. He slammed on the brakes, throwing us forward, turned around and drove to the next street in order to avoid the path of the cat. It was not only embarrassing for him but it also wasted our time.

I never bought into that particular lie but I did buy into another one. My mother suffered from certain food allergies such as shrimp, tomatoes, etc. Shrimp would make her nauseated and too many tomatoes would cause a rash to appear. As a result, when I ate tomatoes, I would also break out in a rash. My mother's statement to me was, "You got that from me", meaning, I had inherited her allergies. So I stopped eating tomatoes altogether, but later in life after learning to understand the Word of God, I broke the curse of food allergies and determined that I could eat whatever God made. I am now able to eat tomatoes without any problem.

CHAPTER TWO

The Atonement:

The Basis for Deliverance and Healing

The atonement is the basis of salvation for the Christian believer. Through the atoning blood of Jesus, we are saved from death and hell. We are healed in spirit, soul and body.

The Hebrew word for atonement is *kaphar,* which means, *to cover, cleanse, cancel disannul, forgive, pardon, and reconcile.* In other words, when atonement is made for someone the penalty for their guilt and wrong doing is paid for.

Exodus 30:10 says, "And Aaron shall make atonement upon its (altar) horns once a year with the blood of the sin offering of atonement."

Leviticus 17:11 states, "For the life of the flesh is in the blood and I have given it to you upon the altar to make atonement for your souls; for it is the blood that makes atonement for the soul."

Since Old Testament Jews knew their blood wasn't sufficient, by God's command, they sacrificed bulls, goats, sheep, etc. to appease Him for their sins. But in the New Testament, Jesus, the Son of God, made the ultimate atonement for our sins through the shedding of His Precious, Divine Blood.

Deliverance: The Missing Link To Sanctification

In Hebrews 9:14-15, the Word declares, "How much more shall the blood of Christ, who through the eternal Spirit offered Himself without spot to God, cleanse your conscience from dead works to serve the Living God? And for this reason He is the mediator of the new covenant, by means of death, for the redemption of the transgressions under the first covenant, that those who are called may receive the promise of the eternal inheritance."

Therefore, because of the death of Jesus, we have a new covenant written in His blood, and a part of that covenant is our forgiveness and redemption. We no longer have to try to make ourselves right with God by our works of self-righteousness, such as doing *good*, penance, sacrificing, fasting, or making pilgrimages to *sacred* grounds. We are made righteous through the blood of Jesus. We are justified before God (Romans 5:9), cleansed from sin and declared not guilty (1 John 1:7), brought near to God (Ephesians 2:13), and redeemed and bought back from the devil's ownership (1 Peter 1:18, 19).

Since Christ redeemed us through His blood, we no longer have to succumb to the demands of Satan. The power of fear of death is broken and it can no longer be used by the devil to manipulate us. His ownership is broken and we no longer belong to him. He is not our *Daddy* anymore.

Furthermore, according to Galatians 3:13-14, "Christ redeemed us from the curse of the law" by becoming a curse for us because He became a curse for us by being crucified on the cross, so that we could receive the promise of the Holy Spirit. This signifies two principles:

1. We are no longer under a curse and the demons of curse have no right to torment us. We are given the ability to reverse the curse.

2. The promise of the Spirit means the Holy Spirit gives us liberty and freedom from bondages – mental, physical, and spiritual (2 Corinthians 3:17).

The Atonement: The Basis for Deliverance and Healing

Because of the atonement, we now have access to the new creation, which is the power to become the sons of God. The Word of God says that "Greater is He that is in you (us) than he (Satan) that is in the world" (1 John 4:4). We believers now have authority over adverse circumstances, power over the devil and sickness, and freedom to serve God unencumbered. You and I now have the right to serve God freely, and express the kingdom of Christ in us in its fullness.

We are now the temple of the Holy Spirit (1 Corinthians 6:19, 20), purchased by the blood of Jesus, which means any demonic spirit is a trespasser, someone who invades or encroaches upon property. A trespasser is also one who invades our thought life, emotions and will, seeking access to our body. God, having purchased us by the blood of Jesus, is the actual owner and when Satan invades our temples, he becomes a trespasser. The atoning work of Christ has not only given us power to be God's sons, but the authority to evict the devil from our bodies so that we can enjoy this life the Lord has given to us.

But in order to possess the blessings which the Lord has provided for us, we must appropriate the promises. This is done through our faith, by waging **dynamic** warfare of breaking curses, and casting out devils. Then we lay claim to that which is ours by our faith-filled prayers, positive confessions and proclamations.

Deliverance: The Missing Link To Sanctification

26

CHAPTER THREE

Oppositional Thoughts Concerning Deliverance

Although the deliverance ministry is a very necessary work of the Holy Spirit, it is still misunderstood and rejected by much of the Body of Christ. This is due to erroneous thoughts created by ignorance and misinformation. Since these types of thoughts can stop or hinder a person from receiving their deliverance and healing, it is necessary that they be addressed. Based upon what a person believes and perceives, he will either, set himself in league *with* or *against* demonic influence and control.

The following are the most prevalent thoughts opposing the ministry of deliverance:

1. A Christian cannot be possessed nor have a demon in him because the Holy Spirit indwells him.

2. A Christian doesn't need deliverance because once saved; the Word of God will deliver and keep him.

3. Jesus never cast demons out of Christians. He only cast them out of unsaved people.

First, in addressing number one, let me say that in the truest sense of the word **possess**, it is absolutely correct that a Christian cannot be possessed by an evil spirit. Let me explain. *Possess* means *to have control of or owning something or someone.* The implication is that a demon has complete control over and literally owns a person. This is not true, especially with a Christian, because a child of God is owned by the Lord. That person has been purchased by the blood of Jesus and bought back from the manipulation and domination of Satan.

However, a demon **can** live in the body of a person, even a Christian, and can so oppress that person's mind with compulsive, obsessive thoughts of fear, worry, lust, anger and rage, that it appears one is possessed. The Christian is a three-fold being, possessing a spirit, a soul and a body. Demons cannot dwell in a person's spirit because that is where the Holy Spirit lives. But because of sin and disobedience, an evil spirit can enter a person through any *gate*, dwell in the body, and affect the mind. A gate is a physical point of entry on the body such as the eyes, ears, mouth, etc. A good example of this is found in Luke 13:11-13, where a woman was oppressed in her body by a spirit of infirmity, keeping her bowed over for eighteen years. The demon was inside her back, bending her over. He was not in her spirit or soul but he was inside of her body. The same happens to Christians who may suffer from chronic sickness, disease or some form of mental torment. I have seen a number of Christians who suffer from chronic diseases such as arthritis, high blood pressure, asthma, and so forth, and no doctors were able to cure them. After praying with them and casting the demons out, they were totally healed. (See Chapter Fourteen, *Healing of Demonic Sicknesses*)

Second, the next thought, which is a myth, purports that a Christian doesn't need deliverance because **they have the Word of God to keep them**. From time to time, I have heard Christians say, "I don't need deliverance because I am saved, and the Word is enough to keep me." Sometimes, it saddens me because I've been there. I believe what they are really saying is, "I don't understand the deliverance business, and I'm afraid."

Let me share my own personal experience. For the first few years of my walk with Jesus, I had little cognizance of any problems with demons. Whenever I would feel that I was being attacked in my mind, I would *rebuke* Satan, and confess who I was in Christ Jesus. I believe the Word, the Holy Sprit and my will kept me from being manipulated by Satan.

However, as time went by, I found it more difficult to control certain negative impulses like swearing and cursing. Once, while talking to a dear elderly lady, I found myself fighting the impulse to call her a vulgar name. I kept hearing the name repeatedly in my mind. The only way I could still the voice was to whisper the name of Jesus over and over within my spirit until the voice subsided and eventually stopped.

This voice would torment me from time to time. I began to inquire of other Christians whether a demon could dwell in a Christian's body. Of course, everyone I asked said, "No". Their reply was, "How can a Christian have a demon if he is filled with the Holy Spirit?" Their responses did not satisfy me. I was still tormented and I knew I wasn't crazy.

Finally, after much searching, the Lord ministered to me through my sons. I was delivered from a number of spirits including, swearing. I finally understood that the Word will keep you in every way, if you do as it commands. Let me explain.

There are basically three things involved when one endeavors to receive the Word of God:

1. Confessing (agreeing with) the Word and praying the Word: This means you mentally agree with the Word of God in what it says about you, God, the coming of Jesus, the defeat of Satan, and so forth.

2. Memorization of the Word: When we memorize the Word, it gives us ammunition to defeat the enemy. For

Ephesians 6:17 says that the Word is a sword against Satan, which means we can rebuke him when necessary. Learning where Scripture is located, and its interpretation, strengthens us as believers. Scripture committed to memory transforms our mind. Plus, the Word builds our self-esteem and reinforces our confidence in **who** we are in Christ Jesus as mighty conquerors over all the power of the enemy.

   3. Application of the Word: James 1:22 tells us to "...be doers of the word and not hearers only,..." This means that we must obey the Word and what it commands us to do. We are to work out our salvation by acting on the Word. We apply the Word to our social life by learning to love unconditionally, forgive freely, give, tithe, help, pray and heal the sick.

   Third, there is another myth that Jesus never **cast demons out of Christians but out of unsaved people**. In a sense, this is true because people were not yet born again. However, the word *Christian* means *follower of Christ*. Therefore, the people who had demons cast out by Jesus were those who were seeking Him to be set free and to subsequently follow Him. A good example is the mad man of Gadarenes who was *possessed* by a legion of demons, yet he came to worship Jesus. Worship comes out of the spirit, not out of the mind or body. Though his body and soul were oppressed (controlled) by the demons manipulating his will and emotions, he still sought to worship Jesus from his spirit. Jesus saw this desire and commanded the demons to leave him, setting his soul free.

   Another example is the same woman in Luke 13:11, who was a child of Abraham and bowed over by a spirit of infirmity. She was a worshiper of Jehovah, a part of the house of Israel who Jesus was sent to deliver. The demon was not in her spirit either but located in her back (body). Jesus made the statement, [16]"So ought not this woman, a daughter of Abraham (favored of God), whom Satan has bound — think of it — for eighteen years, be loosed from this bond (be healed) on the Sabbath?" She was as saved as she could be at the time because all who believed on Him and followed Him were sanctified (set apart) until Jesus would be crucified and then they could receive His eternal Spirit. Jesus, Paul and all the disciples only cast devils out of people who were about to be saved. They didn't cast devils out of sinners who were not seeking God. Just as the woman had a spirit of infirmity in her back, so can Christians have spirits of sickness, suicide, anger, murder, and rage, and so forth, in their bodies.

If we are to obey the Word fully, as it commands, and if we are going to work out our soul salvation, then we will ultimately have to do what Scripture says in Mark 16:17. We will have to **cast out devils!** If we don't cast out demons, then Jesus' statement in this passage, [17]"These signs shall follow them that believe, in My name, shall they cast out devils", is nothing but empty words to us. Memorizing and/or confessing the Word will not cast out a demon; neither will these practices bring inner healing which is a definite part of deliverance and sanctification. Therefore, God's Word will only deliver us if we obey the **whole** counsel of God.

Deliverance: The Missing Link To Sanctification

CHAPTER FOUR

Determining The Need For Deliverance

The Holy Spirit provides us with several ways to determine whether a person needs deliverance:

1. Discerning of Spirits — 1 Corinthians 12:10

2. Word of Knowledge — 1 Corinthians 12: 8

3. Detection through observation — Luke 9:38-42 and Hebrews 5:14.

Discerning of Spirits

The gift of discerning of spirits is the supernatural manifestation of the Holy Spirit, revealing the spirit realm. It is the ability to perceive (see) and/or hear demon spirits in the atmosphere around us. This gift gives us insight into the spirits operating in a person, whether evil or good. The key words are: *see, sense,* and *hear.*

The purpose of this gift is to give us insight into warfare around us and the demons plotting against us so that we can be prepared to do battle, in whatever way the Holy Spirit sees fit. Proverbs 22:3 says, "A prudent man foresees evil and hides himself." Jesus said, "I will no longer talk much with you, for the ruler of this world is coming and he has nothing in Me." (John 14:30). By this gift, the

Lord was able to discern that Satan was approaching and to protect himself by controlling his speech. In another place Jesus was able to distinguish the voice of Satan from the voice of Peter.

(Matthew 16:21-23) [21]"From that time, Jesus began to show (reveal) to His disciples that He must go to Jerusalem and suffer many things from the elders, chief priests and scribes. He would be killed and raised the third day. [22]Then Peter took Him aside and began to rebuke Him saying, "Far be it from You, Lord; this shall not happen to You!" [23]But He (Jesus) turned and said to Peter, "Get behind Me, Satan! You are an offense to me, for you are not mindful of the things of God, but the things of men."

In the same way, we as believers can also discern the things of the Spirit by the same manifestations of the Holy Spirit. The Holy Spirit will show us what is operating in the heavens over our neighborhood, in our homes and through people we come in contact with. When we are cognizant of the enemy's whereabouts, his nature and how he operates in a person or situation, then we can bind, loose, cast down, rebuke or cast him out. It depends on the kind of situation that occurs.

The Word of Knowledge

The word of knowledge reveals information containing circumstances and facts about a person's life — past and present. This information will be pertinent in the progress and success of the deliverance session. The Holy Spirit can simply speak to us and tell us the name, nature and operation of spirits in a person's life, as well as circumstances and the year of demonic entry.

In Luke 13:11-16, Jesus knew the name of the spirit that afflicted the woman (spirit of infirmity), and the number of years it kept her in bondage (eighteen): [11]"And behold, there was a woman who had a spirit of infirmity eighteen years, and was bent over and could in no way raise herself up. [12]But when Jesus saw her, He called her to Him and said to her, "Woman you are loosed from your *infirmity.*" [13]And He laid His hands on her, and immediately she was made straight, and glorified God." At this point the ruler of the synagogue began to challenge Jesus about the law, arguing that Jesus should not have healed on the Sabbath. Jesus responds in verse 15 with these words, [15]"Hypocrite! Does not each one of you on the Sabbath loose his ox or donkey from the stall, and lead it away to water it? [16]So ought not this woman, being a daughter of Abraham, whom Satan has bound – think of it – for *eighteen* years, be loosed from this bond on the Sabbath?"

John 4:7-41 reveals how the Lord was also able to deliver and save a whole city through the operation of the word of knowledge. By Jesus telling the woman at the well that she had five husbands and was not married to the one she currently lived with, she realized He was from God. In verses 16-18, [16]"Jesus said to her, "Go, call your husband, and come here..." [17]The woman answered and said, "I have no husband". Jesus said to her, "You have well said, 'I have no husband,' [17]for you have had five husbands, and the one whom you now have is not your husband; in that you spoke truly."

The Holy Spirit revealed these facts about her life which caused her to repent and believe in Christ. Not only was she saved and delivered from a fornicating spirit but a whole town was delivered from religion and idolatry. You will find this gift very helpful as you minister deliverance to others. By the manifestation of the gift of the word of knowledge, God will cut through all of the satanic deception and reveal to you the circumstances — past and present — that allow certain demons to indwell a person. Along with these circumstances, certain ungodly mindsets that house the demons will be exposed, and subsequently, strongholds of deception will also be broken.

Detection through Observation and/or counseling

Detection: As we observe people, we can tell by their actions whether they are "demonized" or influenced by an evil spirit. The mad man of the Gadarenes, who had a legion of demons (2,000 to 6,000), could be observed breaking the chains and shackles in pieces. No one could hold him or tame him. Night and day he would cry and cut himself with stones. Furthermore, he lived among the tombs, was dirty and had a terrible odor.

Mark 5: 1-15

[1]"Then they came to the other side of the sea, to the country of the Gadarenes. [2]And when He had come out of the boat, immediately there met Him out of the tombs a man with an unclean spirit, [3]who had his dwelling among the tombs; and no one could bind him, not even with chains, [4]because he had often been bound with shackles and chains. And the chains had been pulled apart by him, and the shackles broken in pieces; neither could anyone tame him. [5]And always, night and day, he was in the mountains and in the tombs, crying out and cutting himself with stones. [6]When he saw Jesus from afar, he ran and worshiped Him. [7]And he cried out with a loud voice and said, "What have I to do with You, Jesus, Son of the Most High God? I implore You by God that You do not torment me." [8]For He said to him, "Come out of the man, unclean spirit!" [9]Then He asked him, "What is your name?" And he answered, saying, "My name is Legion; for we are many." [10]Also he begged Him earnestly that He would not send them out of the country. [11]Now a large herd of swine was feeding there near the mountains. [12]So all the demons begged Him, saying, "Send us to the swine, that we may enter them." [13]And at once Jesus gave them permission. Then the unclean spirits went out and entered the swine (there were about two thousand); and the herd ran violently down the steep place into the sea, and drowned in the sea. [14]So those who fed the swine fled, and they told it in the city

and in the country. And they went out to see what it was that had happened. ¹⁵Then they came to Jesus, and saw the one who had been demon-possessed and had the legion, sitting and clothed and in his right mind. And they were afraid."

Also, in Luke 9:38, a certain father watched painfully while the dumb and deaf spirit tried again and again to kill his son by throwing him in fire or casting him into water. It was obvious that something was controlling the son because it is abnormal for anyone to willingly throw himself into fire or water. But we see a form of counseling here as Jesus questioned, "How long has he been in this state?"

As we observe our brother or sister, we may be able to discern their need for deliverance by the following problems:

1. **Emotional Disorders**

Emotional disorders which persistently reoccur in individuals. Examples are:

- Resentment
- Hatred
- Anger
- Fear
- Rejection (feeling unloved, unneeded and unwanted)
- Self-pity
- Jealousy
- Envy
- Depression
- Worry
- Insecurity
- Frustration
- Episodes of nightmares
- Lack of mature relationships

2. Mental Disorders

The following can contribute to disturbances and confusion in one's thought life:

- Mental torment
- Procrastination
- Indecisiveness
- Compromise
- Inability to hold a rational conversation
- Confusion
- Doubt
- Rationalization
- Memory loss
- Suicidal tendencies
- Fear of people
- Bulimia
- Anorexia
- Irrational behavior
- Violent tendencies
- ADD or ADHD (attention deficit disorder or attention deficit hypertensive disorder)
- Headaches (chronic).

3. Religious and Doctrinal Error

- Heresy
- Usurping authority
- Misquoting and wresting (twisting) the Scriptures usually comes from involvement with the occult, Christian cults or doctrines: Jehovah's Witnesses, Free Masonry, Christian Science, Mormonism, Unity, etc. These particular cults do not believe in the lordship of Jesus Christ, His deity, the atoning and redeeming power of His blood unto salvation. Many of them do not believe that the Holy Spirit is a person nor do they believe that there is a literal hell. Any religion that negates Jesus Christ as Lord is a false religion.

If one has heathen, non-Christian objects in the house, they can attract religious demons. Beware of false doctrines, occultism and spiritism, such as: hypnotism, horoscopes, astrology, divination, seances, witchcraft, ouija boards, automatic handwriting and levitating. The purpose of a false doctrine, found in 1 Timothy 4:1 is to cause disunity and confusion in the Body of Christ by opposing inspired Scripture with erroneous teaching. These false doctrines contain enough fragmented truth to deceive a person into believing that it is the Word of God.

4. Sexual Disorders
- Recurring unclean thoughts expressed in conversation
- Lustful dreams
- Unclean sex acts:
- Fantasy sex (unconsciously)
- Masturbation – feeling and rubbing sex organs
- Lust – staring lustfully at the opposite sex, suggestive comments, carnal joking
- Perversions – sticking out tongue, rubbing stomach and thighs, nakedness
- Homosexuality – effeminate gestures, male having female interests and feminine voice or in the case of lesbianism – a woman dressing like a man, talking and walking like a man
- Incest
- Provocativeness – flirtation, wearing revealing clothing, nakedness
- Adultery
- Fornication and any kind of illicit sex

5. Addictions
- Alcohol
- Drugs

- Nicotine
- Medicines
- Caffeine
- Foods (sugar, chocolate, starch, and so on
- Compulsive behavior in eating (gluttony)

6. Physical Infirmities
- Arthritis
- Breathing difficulties
- Chronic back problems (where there is no known cause)
- Asthma
- Bronchitis
- Colitis
- Scoliosis
- Deafness
- Blindness
- Undiagnosable symptoms of chronic sickness.

7. Communication Problems
Inability to control the tongue such as:
- Uncontrolled outbursts of cursing (Tourettes Syndrome)
- Blasphemy
- Lying
- Criticism
- Gossip
- Mockery
- Railing (bitter complaining)
- Jesting
- Lewd joking

Hindrances to deliverance
The following are roadblocks to deliverance:
1. **Unconfessed sin** – Any hidden or unconfessed sin will hinder a person from using his will to be set free.

2. **Fear of deliverance** - fear of unknown manifestations
3. **Fear of exposure** - of a hidden sin or vice
4. **Oral sex** – Some people do not believe that it is a sin, but it is an unclean spirit.
5. **Doubt and unbelief**
6. **Dishonesty**

Necessary steps to deliverance:

1. **Be honest and admit** that one has a problem. One must hate the sin if one expects to be delivered.
2. **Submit** oneself to someone else that can help. It should be someone that the person trusts.
3. **Be willing to repent,** change and be willing to confess your sins before God. To repent means to literally turn one's thoughts from sin and rebellion to submission to God and His way of thinking (Romans 12:2). To confess means to acknowledge to God that you have sinned and are seeking His forgiveness and cleansing (1 John 1:9).
4. **Be willing to forgive** all offenders and seek forgiveness from God for oneself.
5. **Renounce and break ties** with demons associated with one's sins. (i.e: hurt, anger, bitterness, rejection, lust, and so on). To break ties means to cut off all associations with these demons. You must hate the sins that have so easily beset you and you must passionately hate the demons as well.
6. **Pray** and ask God to bring complete deliverance. Invite God's power and wisdom into the situation. Only God can deliver for the Scriptures say in Zechariah 4:6, "Not by might nor by power, but by my Spirit, says the Lord of Hosts." A prayer of submission and for guidance by the Holy Spirit

should be prayed.

7. Be willing to participate in warfare against the demonic spirits.

The minister and the candidate should pray a prayer of submission to the power of the Holy Spirit, binding the demons in and out of the person. Let the person know that he/she has power over the devils so that when they exercise their will and command them to go out they will go.

How to maintain one's deliverance

Knowledge of the following will aid a person in taking the necessary steps in maintaining one's deliverance. They are:

1. Establish mindsets that are conducive to the in-dwelling and control of the Holy Spirit.
2. Establish godly values to live by.
3. Develop a strong will to make right choices.

Renewing the mind

In order to establish a positive mindset that will maximize the operation of the Holy Spirit in us we must have our minds changed to think like Christ. This can only be done by what the Bible calls renewing the mind. Once our minds are renewed our mindsets will not only accommodate the Lords leading, but will also prohibit any demonic influence that might weaken us and lead us back into sin.

Paul urgently encourages us to resist the devil and this world's temptations by no longer thinking like the world but rather, like God. Romans 12:1-3 states, "I appeal to you therefore, brethren, and beg of you in view of all the mercies of God, to make a decisive dedication of your bodies (presenting all your members and faculties) as a living sacrifice, holy (devoted, consecrated) and well pleasing to God, which is your reasonable (rational, intelligent) service and spiritual worship. Do not be conformed to this world (this age), (fashioned after and adapted to its external, superficial customs), but be transformed (changed) by the entire renewal of your mind (by its new ideals and its new attitude), so that you may prove (for yourselves) what is the good and acceptable and perfect will of God, even the thing which is good and acceptable and perfect (in His sight for you)" (Amplified).

If we, as children of God, do as these Scriptures urge us to do, we will willingly surrender our thought life (will, emotions, reasoning) to the Holy Spirit and we will think like Jesus, talk like Jesus, and act like Jesus. In essence we will be conformed to His image and operate in the mind of Christ. When the tempter comes, we will be able to say with conviction what Jesus said in John 14:30, "... the ruler (Satan) of this world is coming, and he has nothing in me." Satan had nothing of this world to tempt Jesus with because there was no inordinate desire in Him. He knew this world and the lusts thereof were going to pass away. He was in the world but not of the world. He sacrificed His own will and desires to please His Father and finished the task before Him.

We must think the same way. We must change our thinking so that we desire and value the same things as our Lord. As we do this, we will be able to wear this world as a loose garment, and maintain our focus in serving God and completing our purposes in the earth. This can only happen by reading, studying and meditating on the Word of God.

Values

Keeping one's deliverance will depend much on the choices one makes based upon their value system.

Whatever desire one acts on, the action brings life to it. The action will produce righteousness unto godly life or sin unto death. What are you valuing? If you were a child of Satan, you would only desire evil. But as a child of

God, you should desire what God desires. You should value what God values.

Are we valuing and seeking those things which are above and not things on the earth?

(Colossians 3:1-2) "If then you were raised with Christ, seek those things which are above, where Christ is, sitting at the right hand of God. Set your mind on things which are above and not things on the earth."

Are we diligently seeking Him?

(Hebrews 11:6) "But without faith it is impossible to please Him, for he that comes to God must believe that He is, and that He is a rewarder of those who diligently seek Him."

Are we seeking Him with all our heart?

(Jeremiah 29:13,14) "And you shall seek me, and find me, when you shall search for me with all your heart. And I will be found of you, says the Lord: and I will turn away your captivity..."

Seeking God is seeking what He desires. But what does God desire or value? The following are some of the things our Lord values:

1. Wisdom

(Job 28:18) "The price of wisdom is above rubies."

(Proverbs 4:7-8) "Wisdom is the principal thing; therefore, get wisdom. And in all your getting, get understanding, Exalt her, and she will promote you; She will bring you honor when you embrace her."

A fool despises wisdom; the wise will receive instruction. The wisdom that is available to us through the Holy Spirit is the same wisdom that guided Jesus in the confrontations with demonic people. Jesus was confronted with three situations involving temptations:

    a. Woman caught in adultery
    b. Pharisees asking Him who gave Him authority
    c. Pharisees question Jesus if the people should pay taxes

2. A quiet spirit (peaceful)

(1 Peter 3:4) "Let it be the hidden person of the heart, with the incorruptible beauty of a gentle (meek) and quiet spirit which is very precious in the sight of God."

The word *meek* means *to be teachable; it is power under control.* A soft answer turns away wrath (Proverbs 15:1). A quiet spirit denotes humility and submission to the Holy Spirit, allowing Him to keep us in perfect peace in all circumstances.

3. The high calling of God (pressing)

(Philippians 3:13-14) "Forgetting those things which are behind and reaching forward to those things which are ahead, I press toward the goal for the prize of the upward call of God in Christ Jesus." A *call to service*: to serve God no matter what is before or behind.

(1 Corinthians 15:58) God wants us to "Be steadfast, unmovable, always abounding in the work of the Lord."

4. Giving and forgiving heart –

(Luke 6:38) "Give and it will be given back to you..."

(Mark 11:25) "...Forgive him, that your Father in heaven may also forgive you your trespasses."

5. The trial of our faith in Christ

(1 Peter 1:7) "That the genuineness of your faith, being much more precious than gold that perishes, though it is tested by fire (circumstances, temptations) may be found to praise, honor and glory at the revelation of Jesus Christ."

(Galatians 6: 9) "And let us not grow weary while doing good, for in due season, we shall reap, if we do not lose heart."

Trial – A trial is, *a testing; proving or being made trustworthy.* God wants to be able to trust us with His anointing, money, and so forth.

6. God has pleasure (He values) in uprightness

(1 Chronicles 29:17) "I know also, my God, that you test the heart and have pleasure in uprightness. The righteousness of the upright lendeth to life."

Uprightness (righteousness) — *obedient acts of love, forgiveness, prayer and giving that respond to the Holy Spirit and the Word of God in any given situation.*

7. The fear of the Lord

(Isaiah 33:6) "Wisdom and knowledge will be the stability of your times, and the strength of salvation; the fear of the Lord is His treasure."

(Psalm 111:10) "The fear of the Lord is the beginning of wisdom; A good understanding have all those who do His commandments. His praise endures forever."

Fear – *To stand in awe, wonderment, reverential fear; great respect and honor for God.* To honor Him above all else – loved ones, one's own life, the earth, and so on. If we honor Him, He will honor us.

8. Broken and contrite spirit (repentance)

(Psalm 51:17) "The sacrifices of God are a broken spirit, A broken and a contrite heart— These, O God, You will not despise."

After we sin, God is looking for a repentant, sorrowful heart and a desire to change our thinking in order to line up with His Word. This pleases the heart of God.

9. Seek Him with our whole heart –

(Deuteronomy 4:29) "But from there you will seek the LORD your God, and you will find Him if you seek Him with all your heart and with all your soul."

(Jeremiah 29:13) "And you will seek Me and find Me, when you search for Me with all your heart."

Our whole person must be involved in seeking God: our spirit, soul and body.

10. Love God with our whole heart, mind, and strength

(John 14:15) "If you love me, you will keep my commandments."

(Mark 12:30) "And you shall love the LORD your God with all your heart, with all your soul, with all your mind, and with all your strength."

11. Suffering (Persecution) for righteousness sake (doing right)

(1 Peter 2:19-20) "For this is commendable, if because of conscience toward God one endures grief, suffering wrongfully. What credit is it if, when you are beaten for your faults, you take it patiently? But when you do good and suffer, if you take it patiently, this is commendable before God."

(Psalm 34:19) "Many are the afflictions of the righteous but God delivers them out of them all."

The reward that an individual will receive is perfection and stability. (1 Peter 5:10) "But may the God of all grace, who called us to His eternal glory by Christ Jesus, after you have suffered a while, perfect, establish, strengthen, and settle you."

Deliverance: The Missing Link To Sanctification

There is a suffering that comes with growth. God wants us to grow spiritually. In the process, we will suffer persecution from the devil, but God allows this so that we learn to grow and trust Him. Some of the things you may suffer are neglect and rejection (not always getting credit for what you do). But God will remember and He will not forget your labor of love. He will reward you in due season. "If you suffer for righteousness sake, happy are ye" (James 4:7). We must develop from the baby stage, weaning ourselves from drinking milk to eating meat as strong young men and women. Then we progress into adulthood, able to overcome Satan by discerning evil and good as Paul admonished us in Hebrews 5:12-14: "For when for the time ye ought to be teachers, ye have need that one teach you again which be the first principles of the oracles of God; and are become such as have need of milk, and not of strong meat. For every one that uses milk is unskillful in the word of righteousness: for he is a babe. But strong meat belongs to them that are of full age, even those who by reason of use have their senses exercised to discern both good and evil."

Also, remember Peter's words: "For one is regarded favorably (is approved, acceptable, and thankworthy) if, as in the sight of God, he endures the pain of unjust suffering. ...But if you bear patiently with suffering, which results when you do right and that is undeserved, it is acceptable and pleasing to God" (1 Peter 2:19-20, Amplified).

There is no getting away from warfare. The sooner we realize this, the more determined we will become, willing to accept the challenge and fight. God also chastises us, correcting us so that we can be partakers of His holiness and become productive vessels of His righteousness (Hebrews 12). Therefore, as we go through our necessary trials and tests with perseverance and to gain perfection (maturity), let us resolve within ourselves that we will suffer for righteousness sake. Then we should submit to God, resist the devil and choose to have a repentant heart. Whenever we fail or sin, we should humble ourselves under His mighty hand, that we may be exalted. The reward will be as the Scripture promises – "After you have suffered a while, you will be perfected, established, strengthened and settled" (1 Peter 5:10).

Use your will to make right choices

When one is bombarded with the sensual, devilish thoughts of the wicked one, a choice or preference must be made. The Word of God says, "When the enemy comes in like a flood, He (the Lord) will raise up a standard (the word of God) against him" (Isaiah 59:19). In order to make the right choice, the believer **must** exercise his or her will. The will is the strongest part of the mind of mankind. God gave us the power to make choices to love Him, submit to Him or rebel and reject Him. He doesn't desire robots. He wants us to willingly love Him in response to His continual love for us.

The *will* can be defined as, *the power of choice; the ability to control one's actions and the determination to act or not to act.*" The will is expressed in our attitude toward someone or a given task. It is the power to consent, submit or disregard and reject. We can therefore do as Romans 6:13 commands, "Neither **yield** ye **your members** as instruments of unrighteousness unto sin: but **yield yourselves** unto God, as those that are alive from the dead, and **your members** as instruments of righteousness unto God." What we do in response to God's Word determines our love or our hatred for Him.

God encourages us to use our will. He says in His Word, "I have **set before you life** and death, **blessing** and cursing: therefore choose **life**, that both thou and thy seed may **live**" (Deuteronomy 30:19).

There is no excuse for us to sin continuously after we have received His Word, His Spirit and His grace. The only problem is a weak will or simply refusing to use it. God will strengthen our will if we use it. He further admonishes us to use our will with a promise of reward. Isaiah 1:19 says, "If you are willing and obedient, you shall eat the good (fat or prosperity) of the land."

The Lord also promises in Philippians 2:13, where Paul says, "For it is God which works (strengthens your resolve) in you both to will and to do of **his good pleasure**." In other words, when we are weak, God will be strong in us. He will help us make the right choices.

Steps to maintain one's deliverance

1. Submit yourself to God daily - Submitting to God means surrendering all and everything one possesses to the Lord, including family, children, worries, fears, desires, attitudes and emotions. (Romans 12:1-2) "I beseech you therefore, brethren, by the mercies of God, that you present your bodies a living sacrifice, holy, acceptable to God, which is your reasonable service."

2. Don't practice sin – Jesus says in John 5:14, "See, you have been made well. Sin no more, lest a worse thing come upon you." This means that if we go back out and practice sinning as before we will only allow more demons to enter us and cause us more and even worse trouble than before (Matthew 12: 44).

(Ephesians 4:22) "That you put off concerning your former conduct, the old man which grows corrupt according to the deceitful (desires) lusts."

3. Walk in forgiveness – (Luke 17:34) "Take heed to yourselves. If your brother sins against you, rebuke him; and if he repents, forgive him. And if he sins against you seven times in a day, and seven times in a day returns to you, saying, 'I repent,' you shall forgive him."

    a. Walk in obedience to God's Word – (James 1:22) "But be ye doers of the Word and not hearers only, deceiving yourselves."

    This means we must read, use, and obey the Word daily: The Word is a weapon (Ephesians 6:17); It is spiritual food (1 Peter 2:2); It is a guide (Psalm 119:105).

4. Stay in fellowship with strong believers – (Hebrews 10:25) "Not forsaking the assembling of ourselves together, as the manner of some is; but exhorting one another: and so much the more, as ye see the day approaching." Walking with strong men and women of God will keep us accountable. The Word of God says that "iron sharpens iron" which means that as believers, we keep one another focused on the things of God. If you stray off the beaten path, someone can pull us back on the right track. We need each other.

5. Give no provision to the flesh – (Romans 13:14) "But put on the Lord Jesus Christ, and make no provision for the flesh, to fulfill its lusts." Do not allow your carnal desires to lead you into sin.

6. Be led by the Spirit – The Bible tells us in Galatians 5:16, that we as believers are to "Walk in the Spirit and you shall not fulfill the lust of the flesh." Walking in the Spirit means to walk in obedience to the Word of God and to the commands of the Holy Spirit in whatever situation one finds oneself. The Spirit will never lead you into temptation, for according to James 1:13-14, "He (God Himself) does not tempt anyone. But each is tempted, drawn away by **his own** desire." Therefore:

    a. Be filled and controlled by the Holy Spirit (Ephesians 5:18,19).

    b. Worship and praise the Lord continually – Practice listening to strong praise and worship music.

    c. Build up your most holy faith by praying in tongues consistently (Jude 20).

7. Be renewed in the spirit of your mind (Ephesians 4:23) by:

    a. Reading and meditating in the Word of God (Psalm 1:1,2).

    b. Memorizing Scripture about who you are in Christ; your authority as a believer, and so on – Make positive confessions (Hebrews 10:23).

c. Visualization: See yourself as the Word says you are - strong, productive, and healed. Use your Word-based imagination to imagine godly things, which ward off ungodly thoughts (2 Corinthians 10:5).

CHAPTER FIVE

Authority Of
The Believer

As believers, God has given us the authority in the earth to rule over demonic spirits and to minister His life, love and power to society at large. Jesus made an "open show" of Satan, defeating, disarming and triumphing over him through the cross (Colossians 2:15). In doing so, He also cleansed us of our sins through His shed blood and made us His body and put all things (principalities and powers) under His (our) feet (Ephesians 1:21-23). This means that all demonic powers are subject to us (Christ's Body) as we submit to the head, Jesus Christ.

The same authority and power is given to us by the Holy Spirit, that was given to the disciples in Luke 10:19 – we can trample on "Serpents, scorpions (devils) and over all the power of the enemy and nothing shall by any means hurt us. The authority was delegated to us by our commander and chief, Jesus Christ, in Matthew 28:18-20 and Mark 16:17.

The Believer's Authority
Authority can be defined as "the power or right to command or act, and so on."

Delegated authority – The authority assigned, ordained, or invested in another who is appointed to represent a higher authority (as in a government, country, or kingdom). When authority is given to a person (i.e., an ambassador), that person has the full backing of the power and authority of that kingdom he or she represents. The individual has all the military might of that kingdom at his disposal.

When Jesus finished His work of destroying the power of the devil and ascended on high, He gave His authority and power to us.

(Matthew 28:18-20) "All authority has been given to me in heaven and on earth. Go, therefore, and make disciples (students and ambassadors) of all cultures, baptizing them in the name of the Father, and of the Son, and of the Holy Spirit, teaching (encouraging) them to observe all things that I have commanded you; and lo, I am with you (my body of believers) always . . . Amen."

Everyone who believes in His Word, is born again and filled with the Holy Spirit is given power to do what Jesus and the disciples did. His power is given to us in Mark 16:15-18; we are commanded to "**Go**... preach the gospel to everyone, get them saved and baptized" and "These signs will follow those who believe. In My Name (Jesus) they will cast out demons; speak with new tongues; ... take up serpents; if they (accidentally) drink anything deadly, it will not harm them; they (believers) shall lay hands on the sick, and they shall recover."

Why? Because the Lord will work with you, confirming the word you preach and the acts you do, with signs following (Mark 16:20).

Weapons of our warfare
With this authority, God has given us the following:

1. Jesus' Name
- Is above every name and every knee must bow to His name, in heaven, in earth, and under the earth; every tongue must agree that He is Lord (our Supreme Ruler) (Philippians 2:9-11).
- Can be used by us, as His ambassadors, to cast out devils and heal the sick.

2. The Blood of Jesus
- Redeems us from every curse and oppression of Satan (Galatians 3:13).
- Redeemed us from Satan, sin, sickness, and death and we are possessed (owned) by God (1 Corinthians 6:20).
- Purifies us and we overcome Satan by the Blood of the Lamb and our testimony (Revelation 12:4).

3. The Word of God, which is...
- Alive, quick and powerful; discerns the mind and heart (Hebrews 4:12).
- A guide to keep us on the right path (Psalm 119:105).
- A sword (weapon) against Satan's lies (2 Corinthians 10:5; Ephesians 6:17).

4. Our Faith (Belief and Trust in God)
- Confirms that all things are possible to them that believe. (Hebrews 11:6).
- Gives us victory over the devil and the world and temptations (1 John 5:4,5).
- Allows us to cast out demons by faith which is actually faith in action (Mark 16:17,18).

5. Holy Spirit

- Empowers us
  - Behold, I give you power to tread on serpents ...and over all the power of the enemy (Luke 10:18).
  - We overcome Satan and the world because greater is He (Holy Spirit) that is in us than he that is in the world (1 John 4:4).
  - The Spirit of Life in Christ sets us free from the law of sin and death (Romans 8:1,2).
  - We cast devils out by the finger of God (Holy Spirit) (Matthew 12:28).

Luke 10:18-19 gives us revelation or insight into the way in which our God-given authority works. Jesus said, "Behold, I give you power (*exousia*) to trample on serpents and scorpions and over all the power (*dunamis*) of the enemy and nothing shall by any means hurt (*adikeo*) you."

The Greek definitions of the above words are as follows:

> **Exousia** – *Privilege, authority, magistrate, realm of rule, jurisdiction, delegated influence, power to judge and rule.*
>
> **Dunamis** – *Might, ability, supernatural power, strength, violence.*
>
> **Adikeo** – *(Hurt) unjust, hurt or do wrong morally, socially, or physically, to injure or make one suffer.*

According to the above Scriptures, Satan's power is superceded by the power of God, which has been given to the Spirit-filled believer. We have been delegated the authority (*exousia*) to judge the principalities within our jurisdiction (realm of rule). We can then bring judgment upon them - written judgments according to Psalm 149:8-9, and displace them in the heavenlies where we are **sent;** in the neighborhoods we are to impact with the gospel; and cast them out of individuals we are to evangelize and disciple.

Our realm of rule is anywhere that God sends us **apostolically**, which could be in our homes, neighborhoods, churches, jobs, and so on. We are called out and sent to preach the kingdom of heaven; to set up His kingdom of righteousness, peace and joy in the Holy Ghost; to heal the sick, cleanse the lepers, raise the dead, and **cast out devils**.

Some people are afraid to cast out devils because of fear of Satan's backlash. But in Luke 10:19, the Word says that "nothing shall by any means hurt you (us)." This means that Satan or his forces can in no way harm us, injure us, or make us suffer morally, socially, or physically. In our assignments against the kingdom of darkness, we have no need to fear, for truly, "Greater is He that is in you (us), than he that is in the world" (I John 4:4).

But with this power, we are required to minister with love and compassion. Without love, there is no faith and no power, because casting out demons **must** be done in faith. Faith operates by *love*; that is, love for God and love for His people (all colors, races, and cultures). So then, casting out devils is not only an act of power, but an act of love.

Things to remember

1. Our authority (power) is God-given. It is not by our might or power, but by the Holy Spirit in us.
2. **This power will not operate if we are in sin. Where there is sin, there is no faith.**
3. Demons must be cast out by faith. We must believe that God has given us the authority wherever we are sent.
4. Demons can only be cast out in the name of Jesus. All power is in His name.
5. Casting out demons is an act of love. Any show of pride will neutralize our power. We rejoice for two reasons: that the demons are subject to us in

Jesus' name, but mostly because our names are written in heaven.

6. We have no need to fear any backlash from Satan, such as attacks on our children, finances, family or our own life, because we are assured that no weapon formed against us will prosper.

Our Three Main Enemies

1. **The flesh** — *sarx* (Gr.) — "Carnal thought, appetite (minding fleshly things); unregenerate; not of the spirit" (Romans 8:6,7)
2. **The world** — *kosmos* (Gr.) – "Arrangement; adornment, decoration (form, ways, patterns)" (1 John 2:15)
3. **The devil** — *diabolos* (Gr.) — "Deceiver, tempter, seducer, liar" (Matthew 4:1)

Our first enemy is our flesh; that is our fleshly appetites and desires. The word *appetite* means, "The things we desire and covet as valuable." The fleshly appetite is always longing for "things" to enhance the flesh. These desires can take to the extreme our need for shelter, clothing and food. When our desires take us beyond what we reasonably need, it turns into prideful greed. The objects of our carnal desires are found in the world. In order to attain these "things," and maintain them, and even get more, we take on attitudes of manipulation, greed, power and control. We are no longer supplying our "needs" — we are supplying our insatiable appetite for more to feed our selfish pride. Thus, we should remember to "Love not the world, neither the things that are in the world. If any man loves the world, the love of the Father is not in him" (1 John 2:15).

(Mark 4:19) "The cares of this world, and the deceitfulness of riches, and the lusts of other things entering in, choke the word (message of God), and it becomes unfruitful." It is through these carnal desires we are tempted and taken captive by Satan.

The world, which is adorned with all kinds of "things," including money, wealth, houses, land, sex, food, power, rulership, etc., is used by Satan to draw us out from moderate, godly living. Our desire for riches must not be to satisfy our own appetites, but rather to please God and reinforce the kingdom of God. However, the Word of God says that it is impossible for the unrestrained fleshly mind to please or obey God. Why? It is because the nature of the flesh is diabolically opposed to the nature of God. The flesh is rebellious by nature. It will not obey God unless forced to do so. The works of the flesh are contrary to the the fruit of the regenerated spirit of man. Galatians 5:19-21 names them — "Now the works of the flesh are manifest, which are these; Adultery, fornication, uncleanness, lasciviousness, idolatry, witchcraft, hatred, variance, emulations, wrath, strife, seditions, heresies, envyings, murders, drunkenness, revellings, and such like: of the which I tell you before, as I have also told you in time past, that they which do such things shall not inherit the kingdom of God."

The nature and lusts of the flesh will go after the things of the world. Satan uses these attractions of the world to entice us as he did Jesus in the wilderness, stated in Matthew 4: 8-10: "Again, the devil took Him up on an exceedingly high mountain, and showed Him all the kingdoms of the world and their glory. And he said to Him, "'All these things I will give You if You will fall down and worship me."' Then Jesus said to him, "'Away with you, Satan! For it is written, "You shall worship the LORD your God, and Him only you shall serve."'

We do not consciously seek the devil out, but we do seek the adornment of the world. He wants us to inadvertently worship him as he supplies us with worldly treasures (sex, money, fame, and so on), and as we do so, he captures our minds and drives us to seek these things more and more. Eventually, we forget God because we now idolize the worldly treasures, hence 'the carrot syndrome' takes effect.

Satan, the deceiver, captures our thoughts, then our bodies, and uses us to sin more and more by transgressing God's laws, thereby separating us from God's goodness. The same temptations he used on Jesus, he uses on us (1 John 2:16).

Lust of the flesh (appetite)

(Luke 4:2-4) After fasting forty days Satan came to tempt Jesus, "If you are the son of God, command this stone to become bread." But Jesus answered him, saying, "It is written, 'Man shall not live by bread alone, but by every word of God.'"

Lust of the eye (covetousness)

(Luke 4:5-8) "Then the devil, taking Him up on a high mountain, showed Him all the kingdoms of the world in a moment of time. And the devil said to Him, 'All this authority I will give You, and their glory, for this has been delivered to me, and I give it to whomever I wish. Therefore, if You will worship before me, all will be Yours.'" And Jesus answered and said, "Get behind Me, Satan! For it is written, 'You shall worship the Lord your God, and Him only you shall serve.'"

Pride of life (ego, heady, high-minded)

(Luke 4:9-13) [9]Then he brought Him to Jerusalem, set Him on the pinnacle of the temple, and said to Him, "If You are the Son of God, throw Yourself down from here. [10]"For it is written: 'He shall give His angels charge over you, to keep you,' [11]"and, 'In their hands they shall bear you up, Lest you dash your foot against a stone.'" [12]And Jesus answered and said to him, "It has been said, 'You shall not tempt the Lord your God.'" [13]Now when the devil had ended every temptation, he departed from Him until an opportune time. The devil will likewise leave you for a while, but will come back later to try and tempt you again, hoping you have forgotten or allowed yourself to become weakened. But remember this:

"For all that is in the world — **the lust of the flesh, the lust of the eyes,** and **the pride of life** — is not of the Father but is of the world. And the world is passing away, and the lust of it; but he who does the will of God abides forever." (1 John 2:16,17).

How are we protected?

We are protected by doing the following on a daily basis:

1. **Obey the Scriptures** (James 4:22) "But be ye do-ers of the word and not hearers only..."
2. **Humble yourself** (1 Peter 5:6).
3. **Change the way you think** (Romans 12:1-2).
4. **Cast down imagination** (2 Corinthians 10:5).
5. **Love not the world** (1 John 2:15).
6. **Seek those things above** (Colossians 3:1).
7. **Walk in the Spirit of God** (Galatians 5:16, 25).
8. **Love Christ** (1 Corinthians 16:22).

The works of the flesh (Galatians 5:19-21)

The Bible says in Romans 8:5-8, "For those who live according to the flesh set their minds on the things of the flesh, but those who live according to the Spirit, the things of the Spirit. But to be carnally minded is death, but to be spiritually minded is life and peace. Because the carnal mind is enmity against God, for it is not subject to the law of God, nor indeed can be. So then, those who are in the flesh cannot please God."

I believe that in order for a person to walk upright before God and live a sanctified lifestyle, it is absolutely essential that he or she understands the works of the flesh. According to the above Scripture, the flesh (carnal mind) is at war with our regenerated spirit. Romans 7:18 and 21 states "For I know that in me (that is in my flesh) dwelleth no good thing; for to will is present with me; but how to perform what is good I find not...I find then a law, that when I would do good, evil is present with me."

The following detailed chart provides definitions of the works of our fallen nature that we call our "flesh." In defining these, it is my hope that once we are aware that our carnal nature is a part of us that opposes our sanctification to God, we will be better equipped to discern between flesh and spirit. Therefore, we will be more apt to fight the "good fight of faith," and walk in victory.

The Works of the Flesh

No.	Term	Definition
1.	**Adultery**	Sexual intercourse between a married person and someone other than spouse
2.	**Fornication**	Sexual intercourse between two un-married persons; any illicit sexual intercourse (beastiality, pornography, masturbation, sex with demons, etc.)
3.	**Uncleanness**	Filthy defiled, nasty, stinking, rotten, vile, contaminated, germ, tarnished, slimy, impurc, lowdown and spotted with disease. Any act, thought or word that is an abomination (loathsome and disgusting) to God
4.	**Lascivious-ness**	Sexually unrestrained, wantonness, unbridled lust, driven, depraved, incestuous, immodest, fallaciousness (obscene), voluptuousness (fond of, full of and producing sexual pleasure), carnal passions
5.	**Idolatry**	Excessive devotion and worship to or reverence for some person or thing; infatuation (dazed and blinded by excessive affection for someone or something)

The Works Of The Flesh (Continued)

No.	Term	Definition
6.	**Witchcraft**	The method and practice of witches and/or warlocks who are in league with demon spirits to work evil: sorcery, charm, black magic, spell-casting, necromancy, Satanism, etc.
7.	**Hatred**	Intense dislike producing thoughts of ill will; bitterness, detestation, scornful, malicious (desire to harm)
8.	**Variance**	Disagreeable, full of strife, bickering, changeable, obstinate, oppositional and aggravating
9.	**Emulation**	Rivalry, competitiveness, contentious, slyly, and openly seeking to equal or surpass, intention to usurp (to take power or position)
10.	**Wrath**	Intense anger, rage, fury, acts of vengeance
11.	**Strife**	Contention, fighting, selfish positioning, struggle
12.	**Sedition**	Stirring up rebellion against the government of a church, city, etc.
13.	**Heresies**	Opinions or religious beliefs opposed to the orthodox doctrine of the Church of Jesus Christ; any opinion opposed to establish belief

The Works Of The Flesh (Continued)

No.	Term	Definition
14.	**Envyings**	Jealousy, ill will, grudging, covetousness, backbiting, spiteful, begrudging someone else's good fortune or blessings; resentful
15.	**Murders**	To unlawfully and maliciously kill a person; to hate a person so intensely that your word and action malign, assassinate and destroy a person's character and reputation
16.	**Drunkenness**	Intoxicated by alcohol, drugs, etc.; befuddled, out of control and intemperate
17.	**Revellings**	Rebellious, abandoned merrymaking, partying excessively and wickedly (orgies)

The Fruit of the Spirit (Galatians 5:22-23)

To live a Christ-like life in a time of adversity or peace, one must deny the works of the flesh and draw from the fruit of the regenerated spirit. When we are tested in any area of life, the enemy always directs his temptations toward the carnal desires of our flesh. There are three basic carnal desires of man in which Satan tries to tempt us. They are:

- **The lust of the eyes**
- **The lust of the flesh**
- **The pride of life**

Jesus was tempted by the devil in the wilderness with the same three temptations. He was tempted in "all points", but He did not sin. How was He able to resist the devil? The temptations were definitely real, and they must have appealed to His flesh. I believe He totally relied on the Holy Spirit to guide and keep Him, and ultimately, He used the Word of God to defeat the devil. I also believe that He drew from the fruit of the Spirit to counteract the desires of the flesh. I believe the love of God kept Him from fear, while the peace of God (oneness with God) kept Him calm and quiet, avoiding panic of extreme need. His faith and trust in God enabled Him to remain faithful, steadfast and obedient to the Father. I believe all of the fruit may have operated in Jesus that day, but the fruit of temperance definitely restrained Him, keeping Him from indulging in fleshly appetites.

Since we believers, have the same Holy Spirit as Jesus did, we can also resist every demonic temptation. Through our regenerated spirit, we can draw upon the divine nature of Christ in us and defy every work of the flesh. Because the Word of God says there is no law against the fruit of the Spirit.

The Fruit of the Spirit

No.	English Term	Greek Term	Definition
1.	**Love**	Agape	(Divine moral love); affection, enduring, caring, compassionate and merciful heart, mind and activity; unfeigned and unconditional
2.	**Joy**	Chara	Truthful, delightful, calm; gladness and exceeding cheer, proceeding from the inner man or spirit
3.	**Peace**	Eirene	Oneness with God; in contact with the spirit of peace; quietness, rest, calming of the senses and emotion, supernatural
4.	**Longsuffering**	Makrothumeo	Bearing trouble patiently for a long time
5.	**Gentleness**	Chrestotes	Gracious, kindness, usefulness; excellence in character or demeanor; sweet

The Fruit Of The Spirit (Continued)

No.	EnglishTerm	Greek Term	Definition
6.	**Goodness**	Agathosune	Godlike, valid, real, honorable, quality of soundness, graciousnes, sweetness kindness; merciful, divinely attractive with an inner quality of beauty
7.	**Faith**	Pistos	Trustworthy, dutiful, reliable, obedient, steadfast
8.	**Meekness**	Praotes	Humble, unassuming, mild, longsuffering, uncomplaining, yet it is power under control
9.	**Temperance**	Egkrateia	Self-restraint in conduct and indulgence of the appetites; ranging from moderation to abstinence; self-discipline

CHAPTER SIX

Anointings And Conditions For Deliverance

Over the years, the Lord has taught me that there are at least five realms or conditions in which deliverance can take place. God's objective is primarily to set His people free from demonic oppression. He is God, Almighty and Sovereign, and can do it any way He pleases. I hope the following will be of some help to those seeking to better understand the ministry of deliverance.

1. Casting out demons by the two-fold faith of the believer (minister) and candidate. (Romans 10:17); (Mark 16:17,18); (Mark 9:14-28).
2. Casting out demons extemporaneously by the anointing of the Holy Spirit (Acts 16:16).
3. Deliverance by the sovereign move of the Holy Spirit, through praise and worship (Psalm 32:17).
4. Through preaching, teaching and administration of mercy (Acts 8:4-8).
5. Deliverance can come from the presence of someone who has consistent fellowship with the Holy Spirit.

1. Casting out demons by the two-fold faith of the minister and the candidate for deliverance.

This kind of deliverance comes through teaching and hearing of the word of faith. In Romans 10:17, the Word says, "faith comes by hearing and hearing by the Word of God." And again, "Without faith, it is impossible to please (satisfy) Him (God)..." (Hebrews 11:6), indicating that in order for God to deliver us, there must be desire, knowledge, and a belief that one can be set free. Knowledge comes from hearing the Word of God — knowledge that demons exist, that they indwell the body of humans, how they enter, and how they are expelled. This can only come through teaching (preaching) the Word of God (Romans 10:14).

According to Mark 16:17-20, when the Word of God (good news) is taught, the candidate receives faith (power to believe) as he hears the truth. Then, as the minister and the candidate exercise their faith in warfare, the Holy Spirit confirms the Word of God with signs following, which is the expulsion of the spirit(s). This happens during private counseling, as well as corporate deliverance.

2. Casting demons out extemporaneously (spontaneously) by the Holy Spirit.

It is not planned; rather, it is done on the "spur of the moment" (Acts 16:16-18). However, when we study this Scripture, we find that what seems unplanned was in reality, wisely set up by God:

"Now it happened, as we went to prayer, that a certain slave girl possessed with a spirit of divination met us, who brought her masters much profit by fortune-telling. This girl followed Paul and us, and cried out, saying, 'These men are the servants of the Most High God, who proclaim to us the way of salvation.' And this she did for many days. *But Paul, greatly annoyed, turned and said to the spirit, 'I command you in the name of Jesus Christ to come out of her.' And he came out that very hour.'"

There is a greater authority here than in number one. This anointing requires no teaching, but supernatural faith, spontaneously given at the moment of vexation. Satan (demon) is surprised, taken off guard when the Holy Spirit-filled believer suddenly attacks.

As the Scriptures read, in Acts 16:18, Paul, after many days, became greatly annoyed with the slave girl's aggravating remarks, and suddenly turned and cast the demon of divination out of the girl. The same kind of extemporaneous power is given to the believer when a spirit is interfering with the work of the Holy Spirit. (i.e., during a church service, time of worship, deliverance of a message, and so on).

3. Deliverance can come through the sovereign move of the Holy Spirit through praise and worship.

Both corporate and individual praise will cause demonic spirits to flee. The Word of God says, in James 4:7, that the believer is to first, "Submit to God, resist the devil and he will flee from you." When one praises or positions one's heart to worship, it is an act of submission to God. An individual's will and desires (flesh) are given over to the "real" desire of the heart (spirit), which is to unreservedly worship God continually (persistently). The deliverance comes as one is unashamedly caught up in focusing one's attitude of heart and mind, and activity of the body (tongue, lips, and so on) on glorifying the Almighty.

David states in Psalm 22:3-4, speaking of God, "But Thou art holy, O Thou that inhabits the praises of Israel (Your people). Our fathers trusted in You; they trusted and You delivered them." The word *inhabit* in Hebrew is *yashab*, meaning to *sit down, to remain, to settle, or marry.* In other words, God doesn't merely come to visit, but as we praise and adore Him, His presence abides with us, marries us, and partners with us in such a way as to drive out every demonic harassment, torment, or bondage. The word *trust* in verse 4 is *batach*, which is Hebrew for "being boldly confident, secure, and carelessly sure" of God's love and faithfulness to deliver us from every oppression as we love on Him.

When we begin to praise God with abandonment, satanic spirits become very confused, disoriented, lose their *minds*, lose their grip, and run (go out), (2 Chronicles 20:21-22).

As Psalm 32:7 states, "God is our hiding place, He will preserve us from trouble and will encompass us with songs of deliverance." A song of deliverance can be a hymnal of praise songs sung from our hearts, an inspired prophetic song or a song sung in tongues. In essence, it is a heartfelt song of great appreciation, love and adoration for God — a song that fills you with His presence (goodness and glory). I have seen and heard others sing, who were delivered from cancer, depression and other demonic oppression while worshiping during a church service, and so forth.

It is very true that a person can be so full of praise and worship that foreign spirits cannot enter their body, let alone stay there. My personal deliverance in this manner came in several ways:

♦ Sometimes when preparing my heart to bring a message, while on my knees, I lift my hands to worship Him, and simply ask Him to deliver me, and He does. I will find myself yawning or coughing involuntarily.

♦ While praying in tongues (interceding or travailing), deliverance has burst forth in me. Sometimes I realize what has come out of me and sometimes I don't. The important thing is, I sense the freedom that wasn't there moments before.

♦ Worshiping God in the Spirit can ward off even the most subtle attacks of the enemy. For example, years ago while working a secular job, one morning I experienced a form of deliverance that taught me the reality of Psalm 23:4b, "Thou anointest my head with oil (power and presence of God); my cup runneth over." During the drive to work (about 30 minutes), it was my routine to sing praises to God. Sometimes, I would sing in tongues, sometimes in my own language, sometimes making positive confessions and telling God how much I loved Him. It always prepared me for the hectic morning at the office.

This particular morning was the same as any other morning, except when I gathered with a group of fellow agents to talk, I became nauseated. I tried to fight it, but it worsened to the point that I had to excuse myself. I entered the bathroom and began to cough and gag until phlegm began to come out of my mouth. This only lasted three to four minutes. I thought it might have been a sinus infection, but I wasn't sure, so I asked the Lord what was going on. His reply was the following: "Those two men you were conversing with were both full of lust. One had a homosexual spirit in him and other spirits around him, and the other man had a spirit of fornication and others lurking with him. They (the spirits) tried to enter you, but you were so full of My presence, because of your praises, they could not enter." Praise God forever! I was so thankful that my cup was running over with His goodness. He truly inhabits our praises.

4. Through preaching and teaching of the Word

A candidate can have such a great desire to have Jesus that he or she draws on the merciful heart of God to the extent that the anointing of grace and mercy brings great deliverance. This type of deliverance took place in the Book of Acts. In Acts 8:4-8, we find the evangelist Phillip preaching the gospel of Jesus to the people of Samaria, to which they "...**gave heed**...hearing and seeing the miracles which He did." "... for unclean spirits, crying with a loud voice, came out of many that were possessed with them."

As Phillip preached the delivering power of Jesus Christ, the people surrendered their hearts to God in such a way that God filled their hearts with salvation and drove out demons of oppression, sickness and disease. This "purging" of mind and flesh prepared them to subsequently receive the baptism in the Holy Spirit. These signs of miracles and deliverance were initiated by the Holy Spirit following the publishing (preaching) of the Word of God (Mark 16:19).

Note: There are two anointings associated with this type of deliverance:

    1) The anointing abiding in the preacher

    2) The anointing on the Word preached

When a minister has been in the presence of God through prayer and worship, he carries a specific message and a specific anointing for a specific person or people he is sent to.

The anointing on the preacher is really the presence of Almighty God, approving and validating the preacher and the Word preached with signs following. The power of the Holy Spirit is present to magnify the Lord Jesus Christ and the work He did on the cross.

"And the power of the Lord was present to heal" (Luke 5:17).

5. Deliverance can come by being in the presence of someone who has consistent fellowship with the Holy Spirit.

By consistent, diligent worship and fellowship with the Holy Spirit, one can become so filled with the presence of God that people will be healed and delivered simply by getting in another person's presence or shadow (Acts 5:14-16; Mark 5:25-29).

Deliverance on this level can involve the candidate's faith in the anointing on the minister, but the minister doesn't necessarily touch or even realize what God is going to do. For example, the woman with the issue of blood in Mark 5:25-30, touched Jesus by faith and was healed, but Jesus didn't initiate the healing nor did He realize who touched Him: "And Jesus, immediately knowing in

Himself that power had gone out of Him, turned around in the crowd and said, "Who touched My clothes?"

This same anointing abided in Peter because he spent much time in prayer and fasting, as we see in Acts 10:9: "The next day, as they went on their journey and drew near the city, Peter went up on the housetop to pray, about the sixth hour." His passion to pray resulted in miraculous signs and wonders demonstrated in the lives of people that he ministered to. Furthermore, in Acts 5:14-16, we see believers increasingly added to the church because of the miraculous healings and deliverances taking place through Peter and the apostles. The anointing on Peter became so widespread that people brought the sick and oppressed into the streets, laid them on beds and couches so that the shadow (anointing) of Peter passing by might heal them. The Bible states in verse 16 that "A multitude gathered from the surrounding cities to Jerusalem, bringing sick people and those tormented by unclean spirits, and they were **all** healed."

My personal experience

Once while visiting a friend, I had an experience which showed me how tangible the anointing for deliverance can be. While talking to my friend, her three-year-old granddaughter came into the room whining and wheezing, trying to get her breath. Evidently, the child was very miserable due to congestion in her head.

If I recall correctly, the child had been sick for a couple of weeks. Without any thought, I spontaneously and lovingly touched the little girl on her head. To our surprise, she suddenly began to cough violently and repeatedly until her nose began to run as phlegm came up out of her throat. My friend hurried to clean her granddaughter's nose and mouth. We realized the child had gone through deliverance. Through the touch of my hand, God delivered her from a spirit of infirmity. Her misery immediately left her that morning and she became active again.

Note: I did nothing spectacular or different that particular morning than I did any other morning. I simply try to stay in a mode of worship at all times, practicing the presence of God by meditating on Him and praying in tongues. I believe that every believer can carry such an anointing if you will "Present your bodies a living sacrifice, holy, acceptable unto God, which is your reasonable service" (Romans 12:1). If you will surrender your life to Him on a regular basis, the Holy Spirit will do exploits through you. "But the people that do know their God shall be strong and do exploits" (Daniel 11:32b).

CHAPTER SEVEN

Other Ways God Brings Deliverance

Part I — Deliverance through Intercession

Jesus is the mighty intercessor.

Isaiah 53:11-12 "He shall see of the travail of His soul, and shall be satisfied: by His knowledge shall my righteous servant be satisfied, by His knowledge shall my righteous servant justify many; for He shall bear their iniquities. Therefore will I divide Him a portion with the great, and He shall divide the spoil of the strong, because He hath poured out His soul unto death; and He was numbered with the transgressors; and He bare the sin of many and made intercession for the transgressors."

Intercession:

Strong's (6293) Hebrew: pâgaⁱ— *To fall upon, to strike, to come between two as a link or bridge; to move God's hand to either help someone or have Him move His hand against an enemy.*

Hebrews 7:24-25 — "But this man, because He continueth forever, hath an unchangeable priesthood; wherefore, He is able also to save them to the uttermost that come unto God by Him, seeing He ever lives to make intercession for them."

Deliverance: The Missing Link To Sanctification

Strong's (1703) Greek: entugchano — *To stand in favor of someone or against someone (devil); to confer with the Almighty, beseeching, on behalf of a saint, and prosecuting the enemy, Satan, according to the perfect will of God.*

Romans 8:26-27 — "Likewise, the Spirit also helps our infirmities, for we know not what we should pray for as we ought; but the Spirit himself makes intercession for us with groanings which cannot be uttered...because he makes intercessions for the saints according to the will of God."

The above Scriptures show us three things:

1. According to Isaiah 53:12, Jesus Christ interceded for us first when He stood in the gap for us on the cross. He took our sins, sicknesses and diseases upon Himself. In so doing, He provided mercy and grace for us all.
2. Today, according to Hebrews 7:24-25, Jesus has provided and does provide help (deliverance and healing) for all through His present-day ministry of intercession. He prays for us, pleads our case and entreats the Father on our behalf. He stands with us in defense and delivers us from the accusations and vengeance of Satan.
3. Likewise, when we pray in the Spirit (tongues) of intercession, we, along with the Holy Spirit, are pleading someone's case, as well as doing warfare for them. We pray the perfect will of God, which brings forth His perfect will, which is healing and deliverance from demonic oppression.

What type of praying am I speaking of? I am talking about strong, vibrant, fervent intercession in tongues. This type of praying is a combination of strong, warlike (energetic) tongues and travail. When one gives himself to intercessory warfare in the Spirit, people get delivered.

There are several types of deliverance that take place through intercession:

1. Demons can be cast out of the person who is praying.
2. People can be delivered from demons afar off (in another city or state) through intercession.
3. Spells and witchcraft can be broken, many miles away.

The first example is *self-deliverance* through intercession. Norville Hayes, in one of his books, shares this same experience. While he was in deep intercession in the Spirit, he found himself being delivered. I will share my own experience. At various times, I have found myself going through deliverance while praying. When I am interceding for someone, there are times when I find myself on my knees or bent over coughing. It isn't planned. It just happens. It usually happens when I am praying earnestly for someone, violently, expressively and with great fervency. Suddenly, I'll start coughing for maybe five minutes. While all this is going on, I may be in and out of "warring" in tongues.

When the session is over, I sense a feeling of lightness and great freedom. My spirit and mind feels pure and clean. I have learned that during these times of warfare, not only am I set free, but the people I am praying for also experience deliverance, either in that moment or later on.

PART II — Deliverance Through Intercession
The second example of deliverance through intercession is people being set free many miles away (in different cities or states). There is no distance in the spirit realm,

for God's Spirit is everywhere and His angels are on assignment to do battle for the saints as God's intercessors.

We need to understand that there are different kinds of angels: angels of mercy, angels of war, angels of communication (messengers) and angels of deliverance and healing. They all have different assignments. Angels of deliverance are ministering flames of fire assigned to displace demons and ensure that deliverance takes place as we pray.

One situation occurred when a group of us were interceding for a young girl who was a daughter of one of the intercessors. Seventeen-year-old Joan had been kidnapped. She was manipulated and seduced through witchcraft. She was persuaded to go for a ride with a young man to his house. He took her home and she stayed there for about three weeks up to a month. We learned that not only was he practicing witchcraft on her but his own mother was also assisting him in this practice in order to keep Joan at the house with them to ultimately become his wife. During this time, her mother tried everything to get her home, including the police, who did nothing. Joan's mom even called the mother and son, pleading with them to let her go but to no avail for they said, "She's grown and she doesn't want to come home. She wants to **stay!**"

At this point, God revealed to me that if we would pray in the Spirit and bind up the spirit of witchcraft, He would deliver her. We broke the power of witchcraft and commanded Satan to let her go as we prayed in tongues. We warred in the Spirit for about an hour until we felt a breakthrough. Sure enough, after interceding, we had a breakthrough of joyful laughter. We also prayed that salvation would come to the house of the kidnapper and his mother. The Lord told me we would experience victory when we experienced His laughter.

That night, Joan's eight-year-old sister had a dream. She saw a demon of witchcraft in the house whispering these words to Joan, "**Stay, stay**". The repetitive cadence of these words drummed over and over again in her mind, held her captive. She also saw two angels on top of the house where Joan was being held. One angel remained on the roof while the other one escorted her out of the house. This was a prelude to what happened in the natural.

Several days later, Joan left the house, went to the store and called her mom to pick her up. She no longer wanted to **stay** there. Her mother went to the house, knocked on the door and the young man came to the door to ask what she wanted. She replied, "I came to pick up my daughter. She wants to come home." The young man stepped aside, called Joan and she left the house with her mom without any incident. Praise God, she was finally set free through the miraculous power of intercession!

How was this young lady delivered through intercession?

1. God gave me instructions that we were to intercede in tongues until we received a breakthrough.
2. We prayed in the Spirit, and broke the power of the spirit of witchcraft until laughter came which indicated that its power was broken.
3. A prophetic dream was given, revealing the following:
   a. The method the spirit was using to control her mind which was the repetitious whispering of the word, *stay*.
   b. Two angels on the roof – one angel escorting her out and the other angel staying to do warfare for the salvation of the house, in answer to our prayer.
4. The manifestation of the deliverance came when the daughter was finally set free to call her mother. Her mother followed through by picking her up.

PART III — Deliverance Through Intercession

The third example involves the power of prayer by casting out demons in another state or location. One night, while conducting my class in the *School of Prayer and Healing*, I was teaching on the "Power of Intercession and the Prophetic Word". My background text was taken from Matthew18:18, 19, "...Whatever you bind on earth shall be bound in heaven, whatever you loose on earth shall be loosed in heaven...If two of you shall agree on earth concerning anything that they ask, it will be done for them by My Father in heaven."

Job 22:27-30 declares that "You will make your prayer to Him, He will hear you... You will also declare a thing and it will be established for you... then He will save the humble person. He will even deliver one who is not innocent; yet he will be delivered by the purity (righteous obedience) of your hands." All of these Scriptures advise us that not only can we bind up demons that are afflicting a fellow saint, but we can declare the will of God and He will establish it, and through our prayers He will deliver even those who cannot pray for themselves.

At the end of class, I called people up for prayer. One lady came up to stand in proxy for her son. He lived in another state. His wife had died and he (a former drug addict) was now dependent on prescription drugs to stay free of heroin. Her request was to pray that he would be completely delivered from drugs.

We joined hands and began to pray, quoting Matthew18:18-19. As she stood in proxy, we called his name out and commanded spirits to let him go. We bound and cast out pharmekeia (drugs), witchcraft, hopelessness suicide, and death. You could sense the power of God. I looked at my watch and decreed his freedom that moment. I had a vision of him sitting in his bed and calling out to Jesus as something went out of him.

A month later, he came to Detroit from Kentucky and testified in one of the classes. He stated that on the exact day and time that we prayed, he indeed sat up in his bed, called on Jesus, and a suicide spirit came out of him. He no longer desired drugs and had a new understanding and faith in Jesus. Hallelujah!

Job 22:30 says, "He (the intercessor) will deliver one (the one in need) who is not innocent in a sinful state and unable to pray. Yes, he will be delivered by the purity of your hands (right standing with God)." This means that you, the believer, can intercede on behalf of someone who is bound and God will set them free. Remember, it is not God's will that any should perish, but that all should come to repentance.

♦ **Pharmakeia is the Greek word that's translated "witchcraft" or "sorcery" in Galatians 5:20, i.e. one of the "works of the flesh." This Greek word is the source of our English words, "pharmacy", "pharmaceutical," and so on. Drugs are inferred. (spcll-giving potion)**

Part IV — Deliverance Through Holy Laughter

Another supernatural way to be delivered is through **holy laughter**. What is holy laughter? Holy laughter is the laughter that proceeds from the joy and confidence of the inner man (spirit). It is altogether supernatural. This inner joy comes from one's spirit man who *knows* intelligently that one's name is written in heaven (Luke 10:19). A person's spirit also knows that God is willing and able to bring him or her through every trial and test and is at all times in direct communication with the Holy Spirit, thereby, consistently experiencing the supernatural joy of living in the eternal.

This joy is not the same as happiness which proceeds from the soul (mind) not the spirit. Happiness is happenstance; laughter that depends upon circumstances. This carnal joy or laughter needs outside stimuli (funny joke, movie, gift, present, etc). If the stimuli are not pleasing, it can change one's mood; evoke thoughts and negative emotions such as grief or sadness. Then one's joy is turned to sadness.

Supernatural joy is always available. It is a weapon of war, and is the strength and power of God. God wants us to experience this joy always, for "the joy of the Lord is your strength" (Nehemiah 8:10). When we are attacked with evil thoughts or words, we can do as God does in Psalm 2:4. We can supernaturally laugh at our enemy, the devil.

Holy laughter comes from God. It is like any other supernatural manifestation of God. It is foolishness to the natural man. It is not carnally discerned.

In the following passage of Scripture, I will show you the essence and the power of *God's* laughter. In regard to the essence of God's laughter, I believe that Psalm 2:4 is very revealing. Verse four states that God will laugh at His enemy, who comes against His anointed. It says, "He that sits in the heavens shall laugh; the Lord shall have them in derision." The word, *deride* means *to jeer, to ridicule, and to laugh at in scorn.* The word *ridicule* means *to taunt, disparage (cause despair) and discourage.* So, when God laughs at Satan, it causes him despair and discouragement.

The word, *joy* means *to have cheer, delight, refreshment, high spirits, and to divert.* These definitions are most interesting. When we supernaturally laugh, we are supernaturally built up and refreshed. Our spirits are elevated and we delight in the Lord. The word of God says, "A merry heart does good like a medicine..." (Proverbs 17:22). But the word, *divert* means *to deflect, disturb, or turn away.*

Let's look at these words:
- **Deflect** — to bend or knock off balance
- **Disturb** — to trouble, agitate, disorder, to perplex and confuse
- **Turn away** — to send to another place; disconnect

84

So, while we are being built up and refreshed, the enemy is being disturbed, deflected and turned away (cast out). In the demons' confusion, they lose their focus and grip. They are disarmed and driven out. Their stronghold of sadness, fear, melancholy, is broken and they have no fortress in which to live; subsequently, they have to leave. Coughing, yawning and tears may ensue. Many times I have personally experienced deliverance through laughter and seen others delivered as well.

Here is how it is done:

In a group setting or class, people are led through prayers to renounce certain spirits; i.e., depression, fear, and so on, and then they are instructed to laugh. This is difficult for some at first because one's mind says, "What is there to laugh at? Nothing is funny." This is happenstance. I tell people that in order to engage holy laughter; you must do the same as when you speak in tongues. You don't need to be *primed*, you just open your mouth and start speaking in tongues. Eventually, the Holy Spirit joins you and your *tongues* change because now the Spirit of God is energizing or influencing your language.

So it is when we start laughing. It seems stupid at first, but if we will put aside our fears of embarrassment, press in and laugh long enough for at least a couple of minutes, until the Holy Spirit takes over, then the laughter becomes supernatural. You feel the joy in your belly, your whole being is caught up, and you are filled with delight. Before long, you will experience coughing and sometimes tears. You are being delivered. The joy is so real that it will permeate your whole being. You will feel warm energy flowing throughout your system. The inhibitions fly away and joy fills your heart and soul, driving out the different spirits of darkness which may include; depression, fear, pain, confusion, doubt, blindness, and so on.

Even the medical profession has come to realize that laughter and happiness can promote healing. It is a fact that laughter releases healing endorphins, which are neurotransmitters released into your system. They promote natural laughter which works to bring healing to the mind and the body. But supernatural laughter not only works for one's physical and mental well-being, it also delivers and strengthens us spiritually. May God grant you His laughter and His joy. May you use it and enjoy it all the days of your life.

Prayer for laughter

You told me in Your Word that when the enemy comes in like a flood, You will raise up a standard before him. Your Word also says, that if I ask anything in Jesus' name, You will do it for me (John 14:14). Lord, show me how to laugh in the Spirit. In Jesus' name, fill me with Your laughter now.

Now, just start laughing. Your laughter is a weapon against Satan. The Holy Spirit will now join you and you will be flooded with His laughter. Have fun!

CHAPTER EIGHT

Necessary Strategy Of The Holy Spirit

Strategy – *The science of planning and directing military operations; skillful planning in attacking and conquering.*

In our warfare to set a person free, we must realize that demons don't want to leave a person's body. Wherever there is demon infiltration and occupation, there is a *strongman* with an army of spirits (guards) protecting him (Luke 11:21). The strongman must be conquered. These *guards* are entrenched in thoughts, emotions and are the strongman's *armor*.

In the passage in Luke 11:21-22, the Lord Jesus states, "When a strongman (armed) keepeth his palace (body), his goods (control of the body) are in peace (secure). But when a stronger than he shall come upon him, he takes from him all his armor (lies, mindsets) wherein he trusted, and divides his spoils." (divide—sever, cut away, detach, disengage). (skullo; skulon) (to flay something, stripped, to harass, trouble). In other words, Jesus and the Holy Spirit, breaks down all of Satan's defenses by exposing ungodly mindsets, years or dates that the demons entered, the strongman's name, the demons guarding him, and so on.

The "stronger than he" is the Greater One that indwells us—the Holy Spirit. "Ye are of God, little children, and have overcome them: because greater is he that is in you, than he that is in the world (1 John 4:4). We as believers are led in warfare by the Holy Spirit, and the operation of His gifts makes us stronger. The gifts of the Spirit that expose and root out demons are the *word of knowledge* and *discerning of spirits*. Discerning of spirits will allow you to hear, sense and see them in the person. By the word of knowledge, you will hear their names or identities, as well as when and how they entered.

The strategy of the Holy Spirit differs according to the situations. There is no set way. At certain times the Spirit will drive out the lesser (guard) demons first and then attack the ruling spirit. Then at other times the Lord will reveal the ruling spirit (strongman, doorkeeper) first, break down his defenses and drive him out. Once the ruling spirit is driven out, the rest will follow. One of the reasons the Lord reveals the ruling spirit is for the person receiving deliverance. It is important for him to know who the strongman is, so that he can guard himself against later infiltration. He must also be counseled to break certain habits and sins that invite the spirit back. When a person understands what demons manipulated him, he is better able to resist the subsequent battles with temptation that may follow.

When casting out demons, remember to do a thorough job. Make sure you get the ruling spirit, and all his companions. For instance if there is a ruling spirit of fear, you may say, "I command the spirit of fear and the whole nest of fear to come out." This may include such spirits as fear of man, fear of dying, fear of hell, fear of embarrassment, and so on.

Different ways the Holy Spirit will use you to attack the enemy:

1. Prophetically call out the name of the strongman, and through prayer, allow the Holy Spirit to reveal their stronghold.
2. Systematically and progressively call out different *guard* demons set up to protect the strongman, thereby, empowering you to cast them out.
3. Torment them by commanding them to tell their names, which weakens and breaks down their defenses.
4. Torment them by quoting Scripture that speaks of their defeat through the cross, the blood of Jesus, and their ultimate place of torment, which is the lake of fire, or the pit.
5. Pronounce the rights of the believer, that one is born again, blood washed, and so on, and that the demons are trespassers.
6. Reveal how the demons entered an individual.
7. Touch the candidate gently and tell them how much Jesus loves them. This destroys the stronghold of a spirit of rejection/self-rejection as the person senses and experiences real love from God. Please be led by the Holy Spirit.

Demon's defense tactics:

1. They try to divert you by meaningless conversation (idle chatter; wasting time).
2. They try to bargain with you (as the demons inside of the insane man did with Jesus (Mark 5:8-12).
3. They try to expose something from your past, who you were or who you are – "Jesus, you are the son of God". A threat to expose Jesus before the time, to cause untimely attention to Jesus and cause a stir or debate among the people creating confu-

sion. In the same way, demons will try to bring up your past (either subliminally or by using the candidate's tongue) to discourage you or to scatter your thoughts with the intent to break your confidence. Also, they will cause counselors to be at odds with each other.

4. Pretend they are totally delivered by faking theatrics, falling down, becoming limp or laying still, and so on. Listen to the Holy Spirit and He will tell you if it is real deliverance or not.

5. Throw them down (*tear*), cause twitching and jerking in the body (religious spirit). Command them to stop or come out; whatever the Holy Spirit tells you to do.

6. Mocking talk or jesting, strange sounds — Bind the spirit or command it to shut up and come out.

7. Fear tactics — Threaten to attack you or one of your children or loved ones. You can ignore or bind them, and command them to come out.

8. Evil, wicked stares to frighten you (especially defiant postures, refusal to talk). Identify the type of spirit it is (pride or stubborness), and command it to come out by its name.

9. Violent behavior (pulling away, kicking, spitting, and so on). **Note:** Usually violent spirits will manifest if a person has been involved in Satanism, séances, voodoo, occultist ceremonies, or has made vows that bound them to demon powers.

10. Running, moving around, wanting to go to the bathroom again and again; drinking water. Don't accomodate these spirits of distraction.

11. Defiant statements such as "Don't touch me"; "You're hurting me"; "Get your hands off me"; "I'm tired"; "I want to leave"; and so on. "I won't come out"; "I've been here a long time";

"This is my house"; "They like me and don't want me to go"; "He/she needs me". They will even openly tell the person that "You need me — don't let him divide us. I'm your friend."

Demons may interfere when you are leading a person through a prayer of forgiveness, breaking a soul tie or renunciation. It can sometimes take a few minutes of binding and loosing to get the job done. Sometimes it can take from a half hour to an hour.

Example of a minister speaking to a candidate:

"Betty, you must forgive your mother," and so forth. As Betty responds, a demon may speak through her and say, "No!" When this happens, with authority, you (the minister), must command the demon to "shut up". Tell him to loose *Betty's* tongue, and forbid it to speak (You may have to do this several times). Lovingly, but firmly, address the candidate again until they are finally able to repeat the prayer of forgiveness and renunciation. Once these prayers are said, the demon's stronghold is broken and upon command, must and will come out.

How does God expose demons through the gifts of the Spirit and why?

Acts 16:16 reveals to us the working of the spirit of divination against the ministry of Apostle Paul. God revealed to Paul that although this woman was giving him praise, she was really possessed by a demon spirit who intended to deceive the people by making them think that she was associated with divinity.

(Acts 16:16-18) "Now it happened, as we went to prayer, that a certain slave girl possessed with a spirit of divination met us, who brought her masters much profit by fortune-telling. This girl followed Paul and us, and cried out, saying, 'These men are the servants of the Most High God, who proclaim to us the way of salvation.' And this he did for many days. But Paul, greatly annoyed, turned and said to the spirit, 'I command you in the name of Jesus Christ to come out of her.' And he came out that very hour."

The Holy Spirit exposes the year the demons entered the person; how long they have been resident; the age of the person; and the circumstances surrounding their entrance.

First example: Stronghold/strongman revealed and broken.

For instance, a woman named Marjorie came up for prayer when she attended my class. She was having problems prophesying, and inquired if a demon was preventing her from hearing God clearly. I told her "Yes," it was possible that this could be happening to her. After she arrived at the altar, it was revealed to me that a demon came in when she was an 11-year-old girl. The demon started to growl and attempted to speak, but I commanded it to tell me who it was. The Holy Spirit made the demon tell the truth. He replied, "I am a power spirit. I control her." I said again, "Who are you?" He answered, "I am homosexuality." Next, I commanded, "When did you enter her?" He replied, "Twenty-seven years ago." Then he began to tell me that her mother associated with a *master medium* (fortune teller) and through the association, he was able to enter her as a little girl. The demon was exposed, and Marjorie, with a struggle, was led through a prayer of renunciation. The demon came out with great difficulty. But as a result of the demon's exposure which literally broke down his defenses, he gave way to the expulsion of other demons.

What's the advantage of commanding demons to talk? Why do they talk? First, demons operate most effectively when they are hidden from one's consciousness. But when they are exposed, their defenses are weakened and they can be targeted by the deliverance minister. Secondly, they talk because they are prideful, arrogant and love to boast. Because of their prideful and divisive nature, by the leading of the Holy Spirit, they will not only expose themselves but also other demons that lie resident within an individual.

Second example: Stronghold/strongman revealed and broken

Martha, the adoptive mother of an 11-year-old boy, named Sean, called me to her house to take him through deliverance. After I arrived, she told me about a disturbing incident that previously occurred with her son one morning, at about 1:30 a.m. She discovered him in the bathroom applying women's make-up to his face, including eye liner and lipstick. She became concerned about his homosexual tendency, which had increased. She first noticed his effeminate ways at age five—playing with dolls, wanting to braid hair, and playing with girls rather than boys. His uncle also caught Sean in a homosexual act with his own cousin. Because of this, along with the incident in the bathroom, Martha felt that his tendencies had escalated to a very dangerous point. She had to do something to help him. Therefore, she reached out by requesting help from me.

Nancy, another deliverance worker and I, counseled with her and Sean to learn as much as we could about his history. He was born in a prison as a result of an illicit relationship with a prison guard and his lesbian mom, who was incarcerated. Sean had been with Martha since he was two years old. She told us that she changed his name to Sean because his biological mother had given him three female names: Vonnie, April and Sherry. She didn't want him to be teased for having *girl* names.

As Martha continued to disclose Sean's history, we discovered that at age eight, another 13-year-old foster boy had raped and sodomized him. He had several relationships with two other boys who made him perform oral sex. At first, he didn't want to admit to anything, but we lovingly encouraged him to talk. I soon realized a demon was talking to him. He admitted it. The demon was telling him to "Run away, don't listen to them!" We commanded the demon to stop talking to him and continued to question Sean. He finally admitted that he was afraid to talk because the devil had threatened him. We asked him why he got up at 1:30 in the morning to put on make-up. He said, "The devil made me do it." I asked him how the demon made him do it. Sean said, "He told me that he would kill me if I didn't do it and he threatened to kill my mother (Martha) and stop me from going to church." He bowed his head and began to cry. Martha took him in her arms and consoled him. She told him "I'll always be with you and I'll never leave you." Next, we began to command demons to come out: fear of death, fear of losing his mother, lust, fornication, oral sex, homosexuality, and so on, but to no avail.

We tried to have Sean renounce the demons with us and command them to come out. Still, nothing happened. This went on for about fifteen minutes. All the while, a demon would make Sean look down or look away with a sneer on his face. This demon was mocking us.

I realized that nothing was working, so I asked the Lord for His strategy – "Lord, we don't know what to do. Please reveal to us the strongman. Show us how to break its power." As we continued to pray in the Spirit (tongues), the Holy Spirit told me that there were strongmen in the three female names Sean's biological mother had named him when he was born. The Lord showed me that his mother had named him after her three female lovers (Vonnie, April and Sherry)! Although Martha had legally changed his name to Sean, the three strongmen still had a legal right to be in him because the demons behind the names were not renounced and driven out.

Once the Lord revealed the names of the strongmen, I broke their power and commanded them to come out. Deliverance broke forth immediately! Curses were broken and many spirits were called out of him: lust, fear, rejection, abandonment and many others. Although we had broken the curses and deliverance had come forth, we realized that the homosexual demons were still in him.

Toward the end of the deliverance session, Nancy was impressed to place her hands on his hips as she commanded the demon that made him switch (walk effeminately) to come out in Jesus' name. It came out. Soon after, the Lord also revealed to me that the two other homosexual demons were in his rectum, a demon of sodomy and the other was in his chest, causing him to walk as if he had women's breasts! All three spirits had been working together from the beginning.

How did Sean's deliverance manifest?

1. First, we all repented of any known and unknown sins in our lives.
2. We prayed and submitted ourselves to the Holy Spirit.
3. We bound up the devils inside of him and in the atmosphere.
4. We counseled with him and his mother seeking knowledge of his past.
5. We began calling out demons, but nothing happened.
6. Through prayer, we asked the Holy Spirit to reveal the strongman.
7. God revealed that there were strongmen in Sean's body housed in the birth names purposely given to him. (By giving him her lesbian lovers' names, his biological mother gave the demons power to set up mindsets of homosexuality. All through the years, these strongmen were able to convince him that he was a girl and should desire female playmates and toys.)
8. Next, we told Sean to renounce the spirits of homosexuality and adamantly pronounce: "I am not a

girl. I am a boy. God made me a man child. I hate you devil. I hate homosexuality. My body belongs to God. Come out of me."

9. We broke the power of the strongmen housed in the three names and commanded them to come out. Deliverance broke forth and many spirits came out of him.

10. The three spirits of homosexuality, in his hips, his rectum and his chest, came out. Then, he was finally free.

Note: In order for Sean to stay free, there had to be follow-up ministry which consisted of inner healing and established new mindsets that identified him with Jesus Christ. I also suggested to his mother that he would need positive male role models in his life. He should also be encouraged to play sports, and to associate with Christian boys within the same age group.

What can we learn from both of these examples? In the first example, the Holy Spirit made the strongman reveal himself to me. He literally exposed himself and other demons. In the second example, the Holy Spirit, by the word of knowledge revealed that there was more than one strongman, and also their names.

Satan's tactics to distract or discourage the minister: Guard demons

1. **Mocking spirit** — Mocks and ridicules, with insincere remarks and scorns, by laughing while you talk. It will agitate you, by speaking in a false tongue, while you (the minister) are praying in tongues. It will also try to mock you by repeating what you say in a mimicking way.
Purpose —To frustrate the minister and draw him into the flesh in order to compromise or limit his power.

Command the spirit(s) to shut up and come out in Jesus' name.

   2. Humoring spirit (distracting) — To humor; to indulge, to carry one along in conversation in an insincere but indulging manner. Pretending to comply, but really stalling or misleading.

Purpose — To get the counselor off on a tangent of irrelevant talk and to stall for time, hoping to confuse and wear him out. Correct response: Do not allow yourself to be drawn into irrelevant conversation. Stick to the task and listen to the Holy Spirit for further direction. You may have to bind the spirit and cast it out in Jesus' name.

   3. Jesting spirit — Jest means to taunt, joke, to do something with intent of making the counselor laugh. The way this is done: demons may cause the candidate to cluck like a chicken, have little tics in his voice, start to flinch their shoulders and neck, rapidly move their head up and down so as to make one laugh. Demons will bark like a dog and howl, and so forth.

Purpose — Demons intend to pull the counselor over into the flesh. Once a warrior is in the flesh, he becomes carnal and ineffective, cut off from supernatural insight and power. When one laughs at the demon's antics, he or she has joined in with the mindset of the demon and is manipulated and weakened by the spirit. Correct response — repent, rebuke and address the spirit to "Stop and come out in Jesus' name" (Call the spirit by name).

   4. Demon of fear (threatening) — to speak out loud through the person, or subliminally, in a threatening manner, for the purpose of bringing fear to the minister. Fear paralyzes a person so that they cannot think or hear the Holy Spirit properly.

Purpose — To frighten you because one cannot operate in fear and faith at the same time. Some statements the spirit might say are: "I hate you"; "I don't like you"; "I'm going to kill you"; "You're going to die"; "I'm going to attack your children or child"; "You can't cast me out — I've been here ten years"; and so on. "You don't have the power to cast me out." When any of this is heard, the minister should take authority, tell it to shut up and come out in Jesus' name!

    5. Touch-me-not demon — In this situation, you may hear the demon speak, using the candidate's voice to complain about you touching him or her. It may say things like: "Don't touch me" (could be spoken hysterically or viciously). "Leave me alone;" "You're hurting me," "Let me go to the bathroom," "Your hands are burning me," and so on.

Purpose — To distract and delay the deliverance process. Command the spirit to shut up and come out in Jesus' name..

    6. Wandering spirit (roaming) — won't let the person (candidate) be still. The person will move suddenly or roam around the room as if looking for something.

Purpose — To distract, frustrate and make the minister feel helpless and confused. Do not address the candidate but address the demon by commanding the wandering spirit to be still. You must say something like: "Wandering spirit, I command you to come here and be still in Jesus' name! Then command it to come out in the name of Jesus.

    7. Flirtatious spirit—This spirit will use a man or woman, but mostly women. (When a man is ministering to a woman, another woman should be present.) It will cause the candidate's eyes to flutter, or make certain sexual movements or use suggestive language (such as making comments about how good you look, and so on).

Purpose — To distract and draw you into the flesh, to flatter the ego, and so on. Make the candidate aware of the spirit, have her renounce it and cast it out of her, in Jesus' name.

Demon Manifestations

As deliverance ministers, we need to understand demon manifestations so that we can minister more effectively. If we don't, these manifestations can intimidate, frighten and misdirect us.

Note: When people stand before you, and you begin to prophesy or lay hands on them, and they bend forward rather than backwards, it is in most cases, evidence of demonic occupation. They are bowing to the glory of God.

The following are examples of demon manifestations:

1. **Burping** — This indicates that demons are present within the digestive system.
2. **Swearing** — These sudden outbreaks or foul language indicate there is a demon of vulgarity and cursing.
3. **Snarling and barking** — This is an animalistic spirit indicative of false religions: witchcraft and Satanism. This could come from generational curses or personal sin (involvement in the occult).
4. **Bellowing** — An angry, bull-like spirit, representing strong rebellion. It will yell to create fear in the minister.
5. **Pungent smells** — This spirit releases a filthy smell and is associated with high powers of the occult and also drugs and lust.
6. **Contortions of the body** — When this happens, these spirits are coming off of the spine. It will make the back of an individual arc backwards. They may take a fetal position or bend forward with a rocking motion indicating buried pain.
7. **Screaming** — Indicates that a demon is reluctantly leaving. If the screaming continues without release,

it may indicate that there are emotions involved that need healing.

8. **Pupils disappear upward** –This means that a spirit of witchcraft or death is present and a demon may be hiding.

9. **Stirring in the stomach and palpitations of the heart or headaches** — This can indicate an idolatrous spirit or a religious spirit.

10. **On all fours with posterior extended upward—** There will be a scooting back with sexual movements that indicate the person has been sodomized.

11. **Coughing** — Involuntary coughing ensues because as demons leave a person's body, they tend to cut off the air of the individual. Degrees of coughing can range from mild to strong.

12. **Crying** — Can occur due to feelings of hurt, sorrow, grief, etc. Degrees of crying can range from mild tears of repentance to wracking deep sobs stemming from hurt and/or strong desires to be free.

13. **Sighing** — Short releases of air (involuntary exhaling).

14. **Blowing** — Bending over blowing slowly as if to blow out a candle or sometimes rapid inhaling and exhaling repeatedly.

15. **Bowel movement** — A form of diarrhea usually occuring about an hour after demons are expelled.

16. **Shaking and trembling** — Can occur in degrees from light tremors as if one is having a chill to violent shaking.

Note: As much as possible, remember to have a notebook and pen handy for someone to take notes of demons coming out.

CHAPTER NINE

Corporate And Individual Deliverance

Corporate deliverance refers to a group of people obtaining deliverance at one time. The group can vary in size from five to ten people, up to an entire congregation of more than one hundred people. The effectiveness of this type of deliverance will vary. Many people may be delivered from the same common demons, while others may not be set free at all. Then there will be some people, because of their level of faith, deeper desire for deliverance, and surrender to the anointing, that will experience much deeper deliverance during the session. The deliverance for these individuals may be more involved and take a lot more time.

Common spirits (imps) — Demons that commonly attack, harass and indwell believers. These include different types of fears — from fear of darkness to fear of accidents — and infirmities such as headaches, stomach pain, irregular heart beats, high blood pressure, rejection, and so on.

A deeper, more involved deliverance will include such demons and mindsets as rage, anger, death, suicide, murder, and so forth. Normally, this type of deliverance will require **deliverance teams** walking throughout the congregation, assisting the people.

Corporate deliverance will follow the anointed teaching of the Word of God. Teaching from the Word of God will define the concept of deliverance; Satan's defeat on the cross; the believer's authority and victory in Christ, and so forth.

Since there is a probability that people have experienced hurt, rejection and anger, they should be led through prayers of forgiveness and renunciation of demons working in their lives.

Revelation of certain spirits will come through the minister by the manifestation of the word of knowledge and discerning of spirits. Before the renunciation, he or she will call out the spirits by name or function. Then together, the minister and the congregation will corporately command the spirits to "COME OUT, In Jesus' Name!"

By this time, the deliverance teams should already be in place, observing who may need assistance.

During some deliverance sessions, either in a class or workshop, the minister will call out certain conditions and certain demons. Those suffering from such conditions will be asked to raise their hands. Then, they will be called to come forward and line up in front of the deliverance teams for prayer, deliverance and healing.

Private Deliverance

This deliverance comes through one-on-one counseling done in the privacy of an office, deliverance room, or home. This one-on-one ministry is much more effective and in-depth than corporate deliverance. The reason for this is because:

1. Much needed time can be given to the individual

seeking deliverance. People need time to talk, ask questions, and so on.

2. The person is more likely to be open and honest because a certain level of intimacy and trust is developing with the counselor.
3. During the counseling session, spirits will be readily identified and exposed.
4. Different mindsets are revealed: godly vs. ungodly thinking. Demons can dwell with one who has ungodly thinking.
5. When people sense that confidentiality and trust exists in the session, they are less likely to be embarrassed and fearful.

As a result, even more will be accomplished, thereby producing a more thorough and complete deliverance. Plus, more in-depth information given to the candidate will help him or her maintain their freedom.

Such information will include:
1) A list of spirits that were cast out, especially the doorkeeper or strongman (i.e., rejection, fear of rejection).
2) How to guard oneself against a backlash (invasion).
3) How to fight the enemy by giving him no place.
4) How to avoid arguments and sin.
5) How to walk in forgiveness.
6) How to sanctify one's vessel (body and mind).

Materials needed during counseling session:
- Pad and pencil for taking notes
- Paper towels or tissues should be used during the actual deliverance session when needed. Sometimes, people will yawn, cry, sneeze, or cough because mucous or phlegm will enter the throat and mouth. During a lengthy session, a damp cloth

may be necessary to refresh the candidate's face and neck.
• Wastebasket

Preparation

Once the candidate for deliverance is welcomed and made to feel secure, the following should be done:

1. The first thing I do is invite the Holy Spirit into the session as *The Counselor*. I ask Him to guide us (the candidate and me) through the session; to take control and reveal all things hidden; to answer all questions; and to empower us for battle. I give Him the pre-eminence.

2. Next, I plead the blood of Jesus over both of us, asking the Lord to cover and protect us.

3. I bind up the powers of darkness and forbid them to hinder us in any way.

4. I lead the candidate in a prayer of submission to the Lord Jesus, reclaiming his or her body as the temple of the Holy Spirit; presenting their spirit, soul, and body to the Lordship of Jesus Christ, denouncing Satan and addressing him as the trespasser that **must** go.

5. I begin to conduct wise counsel and spiritual warfare which will vary at times. Sometimes I may start praying in the Spirit (tongues), seeking God's voice or instruction and plan of attack. Most of the time, I allow the person to talk, explaining his or her problems (marital, spousal abuse, fear, anger, addiction, and so on). While they are talking, I will write down certain spirits that are revealed to me and specific adverse circumstances from their past which opened the door to demonic entrance. During the counseling session, the Holy Spirit will name demonic spirits as well as incidents that may have been forgotten by the candidate. This is called *dual listening*: I listen to the candidate while I simulta-

neously listen to the Holy Spirit (The Supreme Counselor).

At any given time, deliverance (warfare) may begin by the leading of the Holy Spirit.

Setting Deliverance in order (motion)

Once you have cast out demons and you don't see any further manifestations, yet you sense that they are still in the person, do the following:

Once again, forcefully command them to go, and then listen carefully to the Holy Spirit. He will tell you what to do next. If He doesn't give you any instructions on how to further dislodge them, sometimes He will at times say, "Set deliverance in order." In other words, there is nothing holding them there now. The Holy Spirit will further root them out as the person goes his way. Later on that day or night, deliverance will continue through coughing, sneezing, yawning, and sometimes a bowel movement.

Personal example

I once prayed for a Christian brother in my car. I broke curses, led him through repentance, forgiveness, and renunciation. I commanded spirits of murder, hate, rage, witchcraft and others to come out, but nothing seemed to happen. I was a little perplexed, so I asked the Holy Spirit what was wrong. He assured me that everything was all right. He said, "Don't worry about manifestations. Tonight, when he gets home, he will have bowel movements and the demons will come out that way."

I never told him what the Lord said, but the next day he shared with me what happened. He had been up periodically throughout the night, going to the bathroom. His explanation was that the milk he drank that night before going to bed caused him to have diarrhea. I happily told him that he had been delivered by the Holy Spirit.

This has happened numerous times. Sometimes I tell a person what to expect, and sometimes I don't. It depends on how the Holy Spirit leads me. When I am prompted to tell him, the information is as follows: "You will probably experience more deliverance, such as coughing, sneezing, yawning, and even a strong bowel movement. You may have mild tremors or you may find yourself shedding tears for no apparent reason."

I find that when such comments are Spirit led, the people almost always come back and tell me that they indeed experienced deliverance by one or two of the ways mentioned above. The joy of it all is the new found freedom they didn't have before and the bright glow that currently shines on their faces.

Inner Healing – PART I

The Scripture in 2 Timothy 1:7 states, "For God has not given us a spirit of fear, but of power, love and a sound mind." The word *sound* means *stable, sensible and undisturbed*. The word, *heal* means *to make sound, to cure, or make whole*. This Scripture states that God's Spirit is given to us to provide a stable, disciplined mind in our thinking, emotions and choices we make. When there is fear, there is anxiety, uncertainty and indecisiveness, selfishness and inability to love. Hence, there is a need for inner healing to promote emotional stability and divine reasoning.

Inner healing has a two-fold meaning: healing of the emotions and healing of memories.

Positive Emotions

Positive emotions are loving, passionate, ecstatic feelings of warmth, fervor, joy and tenderness. Positive emotions flow from a heart and mind that is connected to the Vine, which is Jesus Christ. The thoughts accompanying these emotions are full of peace, virtue and purity because they are unencumbered by bad memories void of Christ.

Negative Emotions

Negative emotions are feelings of worry, remorse, sadness, grief and sorrow. They also involve feelings of fear, hate, and resentment which can result in guilt and shame. Negative emotions flow from a soul that is fragmented with unresolved issues of anger and undefined pain.

The healing of emotions has to do with the cessation of an overflow of negative emotions that are either constant or seasonal (depending on circumstances that consistently affect a person's moods negatively). These negative moods usually run contrary to the person's desires to be warm, stable and happy. He or she is constantly struggling with feelings of fear, anger, worry, sadness, and so on, when there is really no reason to feel that way. These negative emotions are tied in with unhappy, sad, grievous and tormenting memories.

The unpleasant memories (usually from an offense done to a person or from moments of defeat) keep popping up, causing one to experience the painful emotions over and over again. These memories and feelings can be experienced while awake or while sleeping. The person experiencing such feelings is said to be *tormented, sick,* or *emotionally disturbed.* They can experience physical symptoms such as palpitations of the heart, dryness of mouth, loss of weight, indecision, nervousness, stomach pains, and so on. These memories, sometimes subconscious, bring crippling emotions of fear, resentment, and other emotions that severely inhibit the kingdom of God (righteousness peace and joy) from being expressed in us and through us. The love of God cannot be effectively shed abroad in our hearts. We are therefore, denied godly, happy relationships.

Damaged emotions

Damaged emotions are basically emotions or feelings that are out of place and chaotic. They are emotions attached to our past and to painful memories that are now misplaced in present situations, people and places. We cannot be delivered from these negative emotions of pain and fear until we deal with the painful, fearful and sad memories that keep us from experiencing the perfect peace of God. These memories and emotions create mindsets that house debilitating thought patterns that must be changed. This can only be done by the renewing of the mind which will help us to prove the good, acceptable and perfect will of God (Romans 12:1,2).

Inner Healing – PART II

The process of inner healing is the healing of many painful memories and retrieving negative emotions from negative incidents. It is also the reprogramming of our minds from a wrong way of coping.

Where emotional healing is concerned, you will almost always deal with past hurts, fear, bitterness, anger and denial. **Inner healing will always require forgiveness in four areas**.

1. Forgiving the offenders
2. Forgiving oneself
3. Seeking God's forgiveness
4. Sometimes, forgiving God (There are times when people don't realize that they are angry with God, blaming Him for their own inconsistencies. Rather than take responsibility for their mistakes and consequences, they blame God. Hence they need to admit their wrong and release God).

Demons quite often fill these emotions and exacerbate or aggravate the person's thought life. If one is unable to control his emotions, the walls of his house are torn down; susceptible to evil invasion. One of the main ways demons enter and keep reentering is through the manipulation of the emotions. As stated before, demons house themselves in negative emotions, and maintain their stay through inordinate affections, false comfort and evil deceptions.

Here is the way they manipulate the emotions, intellect, and will of man:

Evil spirits will set up situations of strife and cause people to argue and offend each other through name calling, cursing, or rejection, to create an emotion of hurt. A word spoken, a negative look, or a gesture, can be reasoned out as an **offense** that incites an emotion of hurt, followed by anger and resentment for the offender. If one doesn't know how to, or doesn't exercise his power to forgive, his **will** can eventually be manipulated to retaliate as Satan wills, by striking, cursing, hating, and so on. Retaliation can come immediately or over a period of time, not necessarily for the original offender, but against anyone.

In order to avoid this, one must learn to forgive immediately, so as not to allow demonic entry. Once a negative emotion is activated, it must be healed or retrieved quickly by forgiveness. If this is done quickly or within a reasonable time period, the evil one will have no door through which to come. The Bible says, in Ephesians 4:26 "…be angry but sin not, let not the sun go down on your wrath." This speaks of a progression. One has moved from hurt to anger to wrath. Anger can be a reasonable response to a hurt or offense. But if one doesn't forgive and stop the process, that person will move from anger to wrath (intense anger, rage, vengeance) at which point it becomes absolutely necessary to repent of evil thoughts and forgive. Otherwise, the sun (grace of protection) will go down and darkness (evil) will enter one's body and soul (emotions). When this occurs, one must be delivered because demons of hurt, unforgiveness, anger and rage have hidden themselves in the negative emotions, waiting for the opportune moment to manifest.

If one still doesn't forgive, anger and wrath will turn to bitterness. Bitterness comes from an extended period of meditating on offenses until, as the Bible states, a "root of bitterness" is produced. This will not only affect other people, but will short circuit the body of the bitter person, which can cause **arthritis, heart problems, cancer, and** so on.

How does emotional healing and deliverance compliment each other? If demons are cast out of a person (lust, anger, murder, fear, and so on) without the negative emotions, mindsets and root causes being dealt with, the house (thought life made up of unresolved anger and bitterness) will be open for the spirits to come back. Conversely, if you minister inner healing without casting out the demons, then spirits remain to continue their work. If both are not completed and done thoroughly, which takes time, the process of deliverance is shallow and incomplete. However, when inner healing is done, a certain amount of deliverance will take place because certain mindsets that housed the demons have been destroyed.

How does one minister inner healing, and how long does it take? Just as deliverance is a process, so is inner healing. As a matter of fact, as the process progresses, it will sometimes involve a simultaneous inner healing and eviction of spirits at the same moment. Inner healing can take one day, a week, a month or even a year or more.

It's a process that depends on revelation of forgotten offenses and buried negative emotions of hate, anger, and various other emotions. Counseling is absolutely necessary. The length of counseling depends upon the severity of the oppression, but once it has begun, and there is total cooperation by the counselee, the benefits can be realized quite early.

The following is a pattern of steps for leading some-one into the inner healing process:

1. The Holy Spirit will reveal circumstances of hurt, rejection, anger and the perpetrators involved. Then, a person must be led to forgive his offender(s), ask God to forgive him and, if necessary, forgive God.

2. Help the person understand that Jesus was there all of the time, offering His love.

3. Help the offended one receive His love, for then and now.

4. Forgive all trespassers; release them and bless them because blessing them sets the law of sowing and reaping into operation —you begin to receive blessings emotionally, physically and socially.

5. Ask God to take away the memory of evil. Call your emotions back and choose to forget the memories. The incident will eventually evaporate. If remembered again, it will be like a dream, with no pain associated with it. During this time, crying and instances of anger, hatred, and so on, may occur.

6. You may pray this prayer before and after deliverance:

Lord, I forgive and I accept Your healing love right now. I receive your peace. Lord, help me to remember the offenses no more. Take away the pain of it. By the power of your Holy Spirit, I choose to remember it no more. I detach my emotions from this person, the offenses from this person and I give the emotional pain and hurt to you, Jesus. I receive Your thoughts of love and peace, in Jesus name, Amen.

Since repentance has been established, then one must begin the process of renewing the mind in order to think victoriously. Then a new mindset must be formed in order to transform a person into a strong, stable, loving

Christian. This new mindset not only disallows Satan's entrance and control, but also allows the Holy Spirit to manifest God's love through you. For instance, because God has forgiven us for Christ's sake, we therefore, forgive the offender(s). In doing this, we are fulfilling the Scriptures as we overcome evil by doing good. (This helps a person resist the temptation of giving place to a spirit of vengeance or retaliation.)

When a spirit of fear comes to drive a person to withdraw, or if it conversely draws that person to control someone else or situations, the individual should confess the following:

- *I am a new creation in Christ Jesus, old things (ways of thinking and responding) have passed away, look, and all things have become new.*
- *To ward off thoughts of rejection and defeat, confess the following:"I am not a loser. I am not rejected because God, my Father has accepted me in the beloved" (Ephesians 1:6).*
- *I am His child (Romans 8:16). Since I am His child, I know that He loves me.*
- *Everything God is, I am because I have His divine nature dwelling in me (2 Peter 1:4).*
- *When one has feelings of low self-esteem because of their personal appearance, he should confess according to Psalm 139, "I am fearfully and wonderfully made", therefore, God is pleased with how He created me.*
- *My God thinks only good things about me so I should think good thoughts about myself also (Jeremiah 29:11). I like me.*

CHAPTER TEN

Deliverance Is A Process

Deliverance is very seldom a one-time event because of certain variables that make up a Christian's life such as: ungodly thinking, carnal habits and layers of demons that enter a person over time. Before any lasting deliverance can be realized, there may be several instances of deliverance and inner healing that take place as a result of these variables. We will examine each of these variables:

1. Ungodly thinking

Any thoughts that oppose the truth found in God's Word concerning the individual's perception of God, family members, self and others is considered to be ungodly thinking. This thinking will cause a person to set up league with evil spirits that house themselves in one's emotions and reasoning that will perpetuate their evil work in that person's life and those he may interact with. Contained within the mindsets are inordinate affections that attach a person to demonic spirits that will come and go until their thinking is changed.

These mindsets must be broken by application of the truth to the lies they have believed. Once God's Word is heard and received, a person's mind can be renewed to the extent that the Holy Spirit can operate and eventually cause the person to resist evil influence. Then, the old framework of thinking that housed the demons (ie. bitterness, fear, rejection, unforgiveness, and others), is torn down, and a new foundation or structure of godly thinking must be built. This can only come through the hearing, receiving and practice of the Word of God. All of this takes time. It is a matter of spiritual growth. In the meanwhile, until these thought patterns are changed to accommodate holiness and righteousness, an ensuing struggle with demonic invasion will continue until the person is established in the truth of who he truly is in Christ.

2. Carnal habits

When one first receives deliverance, especially when one has longstanding oppression, there is a tendency to fall back into old habits. For example, when one has been delivered from pornography and fantasy lust and the person is challenged, he may fall back into pornography to bring comfort to himself. The cycle starts all over again and will include the entrance of new spirits (alcoholism, drugs, false needs, and so on).

By stating this, I am not implying that every person has to go through a seesaw effect of deliverance. However, I do know that in order for a person to walk in consistent victory, there needs to be availability and an atmosphere of positive reinforcement. This would include follow-up, word study, counseling and Christian fellowship. The results will depend much on the willingness and commitment of the counselee. Also, it depends on the ability of the deliverance minister to make these things available to people. The counselee should be able to trust the minister enough to seek out further deliverance or repeated deliverance when necessary.

3. Layers of demons

Since demon spirits operate in groups and seek ways to enter people, over the years they have found many occasions to do so. As a result, there has been an infiltration of many spirits. There can be an initial entrance in the womb, and continued entries throughout childhood, depending on the circumstances. Because of curses, one may be led into different types of sin during teenage and adult years. Over those years, through sins of rebellion, idolatry, covetousness, envy, jealousy, lust, rejection, fear, anger, and so on, demons enter and set up league with the person, becoming interwoven in his or her psyche. They offer defense mechanisms of anger, intellectualism, masturbation and perversion for comfort, and so on. Due to this blindness and lack of discernment in what is satanic, deliverance will progress based upon the time it takes the Holy Spirit to reveal and expose these spirits. So, a person may go through much deliverance as time goes by. The more a person is delivered, and the longer the experience of freedom, the more sensitive they become to good and evil. He or she can better discern what is in them and when a foreign entity approaches, they can even discern satanically contrived circumstances that allow entry and thereby, resist the attacks.

CHAPTER ELEVEN

Breaking Soul Ties And Releasing Inner Healing

Just as inner healing is necessary for a person to maintain his or her deliverance, so it is that soul ties must be broken in order to live free.

What is a soul tie?

A soul tie is to be joined together with a person, place or thing through emotional bonding. When an individual is bonded to someone or something through association, the individual has placed his affections upon that person or thing.

Man is a three-fold being: spirit, soul and body. The spirit is comprised of intuition, conscience and communion; this is where the Eternal God lives. The body is the house in which the spirit and soul lives. The soul is made up of the intellect, emotions and the will. When we say a person is soul tied, we mean that individual is joined to someone emotionally and intellectually. There are good soul ties and evil soul ties. A good soul tie is approved by God; an evil soul tie is an abomination to God.

Good soul ties

Good soul ties include:
- Friendship — I Samuel 18:2

- Family (parents and children) — Genesis 44:20
- Christian soul ties — Ephesians 5:16
- Marriage — Ephesians 5:31

The relationships shown above are ordained of God as long as godly boundaries are not crossed. There is no law against them. However, once these ties are perverted, demonic influence is manifested. For instance, where friendships are concerned, I Samuel 18:2 states that "The soul of Jonathan was knit with the soul of David and Jonathan loved him as his own soul." This was not a perverted homosexual love, but an agape love ordained by God. It was the love of a friend or a brother based on trust and godly kinship.

In a family, the emotional bond between husband and wife, parents and children is approved by God. The Bible says in Ephesians 5:31 "... a man shall be joined (bonded) to his wife and they two shall become one flesh." This love that bonds two people together, flows down and permeates the whole family, including the children. This love is approved by God and is for the purpose of knitting the family together.

Likewise, in the Body of Christ, particularly, the local church, there is a bonding together of members in love to maintain the "unity of the Spirit in the bond of peace" (Ephesians 4:3). In other words, the Holy Spirit bonds us together through love, fellowship and faith for "the edifying of the Body of Christ" for the work of the ministry.

In the institution of marriage, there is a bonding between a husband and wife that is sacred and holy. This bond is the strongest emotional and physical bonding between human beings. Genesis 2:24 says, "Therefore shall a man leave his father and his mother and shall cleave unto his wife: and they shall be one flesh." This Scripture reveals the importance this soul tie is to Him to the extent that He emphatically means, absolutely no one is to come between a husband and wife, not even their mother and father. Wherefore they are no more twain, but one flesh. "What therefore God hath joined together, let not man put asunder" (Matthew 19:6).

Ungodly soul ties

An ungodly soul tie is a bond that is sensual and earthly, lacking the anointing and approval of God. Without the approval of God, it can become perverted and demonic. Such ties would be found in sexual relationships outside of marriage. Adultery and fornication amount to an unholy union. Though there is a bonding, it is not pure. Instead, the union is motivated by lust rather than love.

Perverse soul ties can exist between a person and evil companions. The Word says, "evil companions corrupt good manners and moral character" (1 Corinthians 15: 33, AMP). A good example would be a man who has been delivered from drugs who does not assemble himself with godly people but chooses to associate himself with people from his previous environment. These unbroken soul ties, lead him back into the same bondages he had before. This can occur in sexual relationships as well.

Sex between family members is called incest: (mother and son, father and daughter, and so on) When this perverse bonding takes place, the demon of incest will interfere with the child or adult for the rest of his or her life, unless they receive deliverance.

Sometimes people are soul tied to a dead loved one or friend. They are so emotionally bonded to that person that they grieve beyond the time allotted by God. When this happens, a spirit of grief and sorrow can enter a person's psyche and cause a pining away.

Soul ties between a person and a past lover must be broken or else that emotional bond will interfere with one's married relationship. I recall ministering to a sister who had been happily married for seven or eight years but was having a problem making love to her husband. Every time they became intimate, she would see the image of the old lover. After a while, this man showed up on her porch. She wanted to know what to do. We sat her down and had her renounce the spirit of lust and fornication, break ties with the man, and cast the spirit of lust out of her.

Demonic (ungodly) ties in the church

The purpose of an ungodly soul tie perpetuated by Satan in the church is to bring division. Sometimes, cliques (select groups) are formed, excluding all others. Sometimes people are so bonded to the pastor or leader of a church; they begin to idolize that person. When these things happen, the ungodly soul ties between pastor and saint must be broken and deliverance must take place.

They can also be bonded to a doctrine or denomination. Denominational demons have their foothold on a person's psyche through the attitude of pride. A person is proud of his denomination ("my church, my pastor, my bishop, and so on"), to the point that everything including the Word of God is judged through the eyes of this demon of tradition or ungodly reasoning. The person is unable to receive the truth of God's Word.

I once ministered to a whole group of people who had demonic soul ties with a particular denomination. Some had been Catholic, Presbyterians, Methodist, Church of God in Christ, Pentecostals, Jehovah's Witnesses, and so on. I had them all renounce the denominational demons and cast them out. Everyone was astounded that these demons actually indwelt them. There were different manifestations ranging from mild coughing and yawning to more violent coughing.

These denominational demons, with their accompanying mindsets can hinder a saint from receiving new revelations of the Word of God. Certain teachings will hinder them from receiving basic principles of faith, and so on.

Sometime ago, while teaching deliverance, a dear lady began to growl (demonically) and bow her head, something she did every week. This particular day, it happened several times. Finally, I called her to the pulpit and ministered to her. As I challenged the demon that was manifesting after much resistance, I asked the Holy Spirit "Who is he?" By the word of knowledge, I heard these words, "spirit of the Baptist." Prior to the day of her deliverance, she had tried many times to leave her particular church, but the demon would lead her back. His job was to keep her bound to a denominational doctrine that inferred, "Born Baptist, bred Baptist and will always be a Baptist". This demon kept her from receiving revelation of the word of faith for healing and deliverance. Once the woman renounced the denominational demon and it was cast out, she was able to receive all of God's Word and is now a strong woman of God who operates in the healing and deliverance ministry.

Note: I am not inferring that the teachings of the Baptist faith are opposed to the revelation of Jesus Christ but there are certain teachings of many denominational groups that oppose the ministry of deliverance.

The following is a prayer to renounce denominational demons:

Father, I have had my pastor in a place of reverence that interferes with my reverence of you. I have put more trust in him than I have in you. Please forgive me. I will put no other god before you. I now break ungodly ties with Pastor_____. I break the emotional bonds and every unholy vow I made in my heart or otherwise. I sever this tie in Jesus' name.

I have placed more emphasis on this church / denomination than I have on the Word of God. This is error and it is sin. Please forgive me Father, in Jesus' name. I now break ties with any erroneous doctrine or any tradition of man and I cling to the word of God in communion with the Holy Spirit.

I break every soul tie with the denominational / religious spirit of (name of denomination or religious organization).

Breaking soul ties

1. Make sure that the candidate is ready and willing to break ungodly soul ties with the other individual.
2. Next, the candidate must make the pronounce ment that he or she doesn't want to be tied to the individual any longer.
3. One must actually make a declaration calling the person's name and saying, "I release you from every unholy vow you made to me and I made to you. I now release you and I take back my affections and emotions. " (This doesn't mean that the candidate must be present with the other person. Rather, it should be done privately.)
4. The candidate should ask God to sever all emotional ties with the other person or erroneous doctrine.
5. Whenever there is an unholy union, regardless of the type of relationship, there is demonic involvement. Therefore, every demon that was involved in the relationship must be renounced and cast out. This would include denominational demons.

Prayer that should be prayed by the candidate, to break ungodly soul ties:

Father, I realize that this relationship was unholy and inordinate. I know that I bound myself to a sinful situation with _____. I want to be free of this unholy bond, therefore, I ask you to forgive me and cleanse me from the sin of idolatry. Lord I ask you to give me power to sever this relationship. I choose to sever this relationship with _____ and I let _____ go. _____,I release you from every vow you made to me and I release you from any soul tie that was made with me. I ask you Lord to forgive me of every unholy vow I made and sever this relationship right now, in Jesus name. I choose to forget every negative image and I ask you to heal my memory. I take back my affections and I give them to you, Father. I break ties with every demon associated with this affair. Spirit of fornication, lust, deception, self-deception, "Come out of me in Jesus' mighty name! I command you to go!

How To Release Inner Healing

As stated previously in chapter 9, *Corporate and Individual Deliverance*, "the process of inner healing is the healing of many painful memories and retrieving negative emotions from negative incidents." After praying the prayer of inner healing and releasing the anointing, the process of inner healing will come after a period of time. God, in His mercy, tenderly brings to mind negative incidents in order to give the individual opportunities to forgive their offender. This is a gradual process giving the person time to heal, little by little. Sometimes, certain painful memories may briefly arise followed by the Holy Spirit's whispers, "forgive her" or "release him." As the person obediently forgives, he will experience the healing touch of the Father.

The following prayer should be prayed *with* the minister to release inner healing:

Father, please heal my emotions and deliver me from these painful memories. Heal my heart of all the pain, guilt and shame that came with these moments of hurt. I no longer want to remember ugly incidents with _____.
I forgive _____and release _____.
I take back my emotions. Thank you Lord. I prepare my heart for the redemptive working of the Holy Spirit in my soul, in Jesus' name, Amen.

CHAPTER TWELVE

Understanding Curses And How To Break Them

At one time or another, every deliverance ministry must deal with curses over people's lives. Demons and curses go hand in hand. As deliverance ministers, we should have an understanding of curses and how they affect people and how to break them. In this chapter, we will deal with both.

What is a curse?
A state of being in which the blessings (favor, honor) of God are absent. There is also the prevalent manifestation of evil; chronic sickness, poverty, social disenfranchisement, mental illness, constant harassment, divorce, breakdown of family relationships, chronic failures, impotence, barrenness, spiritual deafness and spiritual blindness, and so on.

The biblical definition of a curse is taken from the Hebrew word, *arar*. It means *to utter a wish of evil against someone or to call for mischief, harm and injury to fall on a person, place or thing.*

The literal definition of curse is, "living in a state of evil or harm, torment, or a wretched, detestable state."

125

In the following section explaining laws governing curses, you will learn that demons are agents that perpetuate all curses. These demons are called familiar spirits.

Familiar Spirits

An evil, wicked generational demon—has generational knowledge of a family—that is, familiar (intimately involved) with a family or individual. The spirit has come down through the blood line of a family; has traveled through and used individuals of the family for generations. These spirits perpetuate curses, wickedness, and certain sicknesses peculiar to a particular family. Some of the things they perpetuate are insanity, incest, fears, criminality, incarceration, witchcraft, Satanism, poverty, different types of allergies and diseases, early death, adultery, fornication, fortune telling, and so on.

The word *familiar* denotes intimacy. In other words, the familiar spirit has intimate knowledge of the family line. These spirits perpetuate certain sins through the reinforcement of certain mindsets through traditions (superstitions and lies) taught by parents and other family members. Because of the sins of forefathers, and the continuation of those sins through each generation, a perpetual door is left open and they enter at will.

Familiar spirits collaborate with other spirits in the family and community to create situations conducive to the manipulation of an individual to commit the same sins that previous generations committed. Their aim is to not only perpetuate the old sins in the present generation, but to create new ones, in order to ensure the spread of a greater curse in the following generation. The cycle of sin must be broken so that grace will be released to the current and next generation. The only way they can be stopped is through salvation, curse-breaking and deliverance.

Truths to be considered

1. Curses are real and set in motion by God as judgment for man's sins.

(Deuteronomy 28:15) "But it shall come to pass, if you do not obey the voice of the Lord your God, to observe carefully all His commandments . . . all these curses will come upon you and overtake you."

2. The reason for a curse is because of:

a. The law of sowing and reaping—The spiritual law of sowing and reaping regulates a curse. When one sins against God's commandments, it will bring a reciprocation of deeds done. If a person lies, he will be lied upon. If one slanders others, then one will be slandered. The same way God promises a reward for obedience (Deuteronomy 28:12), He also promises to punish sin with a curse for the law of sin is death.

b. Disobedience to the commandments of God will activate the law of sin and death. In the same way that God rewards obedience (Deuteronomy 28:12); He will also recompense sins with a curse. When we sin, we open the door to a curse, for the Bible says, in Proverbs 26:2: "Like a fluttering sparrow or a darting swallow, a curse does not come to rest without a cause." Genesis 3:14-17 shows a three-fold curse of disobedience: the snake, Adam and Eve. The curse upon the snake was a transformation from walking upright to crawling on its belly (he either walked upright or flew). It was cursed because it allowed Satan to use it. God said to the serpent, "Because you have done this, you are cursed more than all cattle, and more than every beast of the field; on your belly you shall go, and you shall eat dust all the days of your life" (Genesis 3:14).

Eve was also cursed with an increase in pain during child-bearing and she was to be subject to Adam, her husband. (Genesis 3:16) God said to Eve: "I will greatly multiply your sorrow and your conception. In pain you shall bring forth children; your desire shall be for your husband, and he shall rule over you."

Adam was subjected to painful labor, working by the sweat of his brow in order to eat. The ground was also cursed because of his transgression (Genesis 3:17). God said to Adam, "Because you have heeded the voice of your wife, and have eaten from the tree of which I commanded you, saying 'you shall not eat of it': Cursed is the ground for your sake; in toil you shall eat it all the days of your life. Both thorns and thistles it shall bring forth for you... in the sweat of your face you shall eat bread until you return to the ground..."

3. Curses are operated by demon spirits who lurk about, waiting for us to disobey the law of God so they can attack us. Because sin is a spiritual thing, curses are spiritual as well. Just as you cannot cure sin except by the blood of Jesus, neither can you cure a curse by natural means. In Ephesians 4:26,27, we are instructed not to give place to the devil. Giving place to Satan is allowing him to take hold of our minds (thoughts and reasoning) because of our refusal to forgive or stop sinning. Sin blinds us and we are taken captive by Satan at his will.

4. If a person is unrepentant and continues in sin there is nothing that can be done for them. The demons of curse will remain and so will the curse. But if we will obey the Word of God, and seek His forgiveness, God will see to it that our redemption and sanctification is complete. (1 John 1: 8-9) "If we say we have no sin we deceive ourselves, and the truth is not in us. If we confess our sins, He is faithful and just to forgive us our sins, and to cleanse us from all unrighteousness."

5. The curse of the law has been broken. The graceless law of the Old Testament does not condemn us if we are in Christ Jesus. Under the old covenant once a curse was imposed it would surely come to pass. Because of King David's sin against Uriah and his adulterous affair with Bathsheba, there was a curse pronounced over his family. He had Uriah killed, so the spirit of murder came into his family through his son, Absalom. Subsequently,

Absalom killed his brother, fornicated with his father's concubines and tried to take the kingdom from David (2 Samual 12:10,11,14). Thus, the curse was fulfilled. But due to the blood of Jesus, new covenant believers are no longer under the curse of the law, according to Galatians 3:13, Christ has **redeemed us** from every curse.

6. We must appropriate our redemption. Though the blessings have been provided for us, we must do our part by laying hold of what is ours. We must seize our redemption by our faith-filled prayers and declarations. We must claim what is ours by breaking the curses, and casting out the demon of curse.

Note: You will find the steps for breaking curses at the end of this chapter.

TYPES OF CURSES
Generational Curses

Generational curses are those which come down from ancestors' transgressions and sins through the family bloodline.

(Exodus 34:6,7) ". . . keeping mercy for thousands, forgiving iniquity and transgressions and sins, by no means clearing the guilty, visiting the iniquity of the fathers upon the children and the children's children, to the third and fourth generation."

Deuteronomy 28:1-14 names all the blessings that will come upon us if we obey the voice of God. We are promised to be blessed wherever we go; our children will be blessed, our finances (in the home and out), protection from our enemies, prosperity in our industry, a wonderful covenant relationship with God, heavenly blessings, exaltation before nations (people), and so on. In the same way, He declares curses upon all who disobey and willfully transgress His laws. The curses will come upon his descendants (Deuteronomy 28:15-68). In this chapter, far more curses than blessings are named.

Curses: Include poverty, perpetual financial insufficiency, barrenness, impotency, miscarriages, female problems, failure, procrastination, inability to complete projects, untimely and premature death, sickness, disease (both chronic and hereditary), life traumas (crisis to crisis), mental, emotional breakdown, inability to retain God's Word, lack of desire to read the Word, spiritual blindness and deafness, social disenfranchisement, rejection, dejection, and so on...

Barrenness: Example of a Generational Curse

A young couple came to the *School of Prayer & Healing* seeking help for barrenness. They had been medically tested and both of them were healthy enough to produce children. As they stood before me I was reminded of Hannah, the mother of Samuel who was ridiculed because she could not have a child for her husband. In her desperation, she went to the prophet Eli seeking prayer. As the story goes, Eli prayed for her and God gave her a son.

1 Samuel 1:1-2; 6-20

[1] "Now there was a certain man of Ramathaim Zophim, of the mountains of Ephraim, and his name was Elkanah the son of Jeroham, the son of Elihuthe son of Tohu, the son of Zuph, an Ephraimite. [2] And he had two wives: the name of one was Hannah, and the name of the other Peninnah. Peninnah had children, but Hannah had no children. [6] And her rival also provoked her severely, to make her miserable, because the LORD had closed her womb. [7] So it was, year by year, when she went up to the house of the LORD, that she provoked her; therefore she wept and did not eat. [8] Then Elkanah her husband said to her, "Hannah, why do you weep? Why do you not eat? And why is your heart grieved? Am I not better to you than ten sons?" [9] So Hannah arose after they had finished eating and drinking in Shiloh. Now Eli the priest was

sitting on the seat by the doorpost of the tabernacle of the LORD. ¹⁰And she was in bitterness of soul, and prayed to the LORD and wept in anguish. ¹¹Then she made a vow and said, "O Lord of hosts, if You will indeed look on the affliction of Your maidservant and remember me, and not forget Your maidservant, but will give your maidservant a male child, then I will give him to the LORD all the days of his life, and no razor shall come upon his head." ¹²And it happened, as she continued praying before the LORD, that Eli watched her mouth. ¹³Now Hannah spoke in her heart; only her lips moved, but her voice was not heard. Therefore Eli thought she was drunk. ¹⁴So Eli said to her, "How long will you be drunk? Put your wine away from you!" ¹⁵But Hannah answered and said, "No, my lord, I am a woman of sorrowful spirit. I have drunk neither wine nor intoxicating drink, but have poured out my soul before the LORD. ¹⁶Do not consider your maidservant a wicked woman, for out of the abundance of my complaint and grief I have spoken until now." ¹⁷Then Eli answered and said, "Go in peace, and the God of Israel grant your petition which you have asked of Him." ¹⁸And she said, "Let your maidservant find favor in your sight." So the woman went her way and ate, and her face was no longer sad. ¹⁹Then they rose early in the morning and worshiped before the LORD, and returned and came to their house at Ramah. And Elkanah knew Hannah his wife, and the LORD remembered her. ²⁰So it came to pass in the process of time that Hannah conceived and bore a son, and called his name Samuel, saying, "Because I have asked for him from the LORD."

The couple standing before me had tried again and again to have a child to no avail. Before I prayed for them, I advised them that the barrenness was a curse and had to be broken. Just as Hannah had promised the Lord she would dedicate Samuel to God, I had this couple dedicate the child they desired unto the Lord.

First, I had them both place their hands on the woman's stomach and dedicate the child to the Lord. Secondly, I laid my hand over their hands and broke the curses of barrenness over her. Thirdly, I commanded the spirit of barrenness to come out. Finally, I commanded her womb to *open* and receive *life.*

The following year, she gave birth to their first child. Since then, she birthed **four more** children into the world. Praise Jesus!

Personal Sin Curses (Disobedience)

A personal sin curse is blatant disobedience to God's Word or commands. It can be done willfully or ignorantly. When one continues in this state, he or she brings a curse upon themselves.

(Deuteronomy 27:26) "Cursed is the man who does not uphold the words of this law by carrying them out." This is outright disobedience to the commandments or Word of God.

A sin of commission is when one commits an act of transgression of God's law. A sin of omission is when one omits (refuses) to act in obedience to God's command.

Cursed acts are found in Deuteronomy 27:15-26. The results of these acts of disobedience are stated in Deuteronomy 28:15-68. Also, refusing to give tithes and offerings unto the Lord can bring a curse of poverty, sickness, and so forth (Malachi 3:8-9).

Miscarriage: Example of a Personal Sin Curse

Melanie, a young lady raised in a Christian family, had several, at least three miscarriages. She kept trying to have children, but to no avail. The problem with Melanie was that she was not married! She had been impregnated by several different men in her life.

Over the years, I tried to warn her that fornication was a sin and her womb was cursed because of her disobedience. The Word tells us in Romans 6:23 that "The wages of sin is death". Each time Melanie became pregnant, she would lose her baby near the end of the first trimester.

I kept encouraging her to repent, get back in church and marry the man she loved. Finally, she agreed to marry the father of her last unborn child.

One evening, I went by her family's home and prayed with her. First, I encouraged her to repent and to seek God's forgiveness. Then, I pleaded the blood of Jesus over her body as she rededicated her body to the Holy Spirit. Third, I broke the sin curse over her and commanded three spirits to come out of her:

1. Breach birth
2. Miscarriage
3. Death

Afterward, immediate freedom and joy was released in her spirit. When I last saw her, she was married and had five beautiful children.

Abortion (murder)

Abortion is another example of a personal sin curse. It is defined as the expulsion of a fetus before it is able to survive, especially if purposely induced. Since abortion is so prevalent today, both in the Body of Christ and in the world, as a deliverance minister, one will have to deal with healing those who have participated in the act. The ramifications of this atrocious act are far reaching, causing all kinds of problems in the child of God.

Abortion is a sin because it is an act of murder. The world around us, namely "pro-choice" people, don't consider it sin. They assert that a fetus is not a life, and a woman owns her own body, therefore she has a right to choose whether her baby lives or dies. On the contrary, a woman does not own her body (1 Corinthians 6:19), God does. She does have a free will and can choose life or death, hell or heaven, but not without consequences. Abortion has consequences.

In God's eyes, a fetus is a life. It is the beginning stages of a baby (a soul). God breathes life into it; it is therefore a living soul. To abort this life is **murder,** and everyone who does it comes under the sway (curse) of the Phoenician god, Molech. This demon requires the sacrifice of children (see Leviticus 20:2-3). To commit such a sin is to invite a spirit of death into one's life. For God declared in Leviticus 20:13, that those who commit such an abomination "shall be put to death."

When a woman agrees to the death of her fetus, she sets in motion the law of sowing and reaping. Because she has brought death to her baby, she in turn receives a spirit of death and murder into her womb. These demons will lodge there and proceed to destroy the female parts and bring pain to the back as well. Only the grace of God prevents total havoc to the person's body.

These spirits will even cause miscarriages, breach births, barreness, and pain in the stomach, back and head. These demons of infirmity will dwell there until cast out. Many times, the door has been opened to other spirits that perpetuate negative emotions such as guilt, shame, grief and sorrow. A woman under the sway of these spirits can suffer with troubled thinking, a crippled personality, and her ability to be a healthy worshiper is greatly impeded. However, when these demons are cast out she will experience the love and intimacy with Christ she was created for.

When praying for a woman who has committed the act of abortion, you must show love and compassion. She must be led through a prayer of repentance (which is acknowledging the sin and turning away from it). Second, she must ask God for forgiveness, and in the process, forgive others who participated in it. Third, because of grief and guilt associated with abortion, the mother should ask the baby (now in heaven) to forgive her, expressing godly sorrow. Then, she is to release the child to God.

Other demons that may come out are fear of exposure, self-condemnation, guilt and shame. Other possible spirits of infirmities are cancer, deterioration of ovaries and the womb. After the demons are cast out, one should pray for healing to take place.

Prayer of deliverance for abortion:
"Father, I admit that committing abortion was sinful and an act of murder. I am sorry and I ask your forgiveness in Jesus' name. Forgive me for killing my baby(ies). I receive your forgiveness. I ask the baby to forgive me and I release my child (children) who is with you in heaven. Now Lord, I renounce the spirit of death, murder, suicide (if it's there), guilt and shame. I command you to come out of me, now, in Jesus' name!"

If you sense any of the above mentioned infirmities, then pray the following:
I command the spirit of cancer, deterioration of ovaries, the womb, and so on, to come out in Jesus' name.

After deliverance is completed, then pray the following:
Father, I release your healing power into this person. I take authority over any sickness, disease or damage perpetrated by these demons. I release healing in Jesus' name.

The Accursed thing
Accursed things are actually idols or objects of worship to another deity or false god. The following examples from the Word of God reveal warnings and consequences for accepting accursed things:

(Romans 1:23) "And changed the glory of the incorruptible God into an image made like to corruptible man, and to birds, and four-footed beasts, and creeping things."

(Joshua 7:1) "But the children of Israel committed a trespass in the accursed thing: for Achan, the son of Carmi, the son of Zabdi, the son of Zerah, of the tribe of Judah, took of the accursed thing: and the anger of the LORD was kindled against the children of Israel."

(Exodus 20:4) "You shall not make for yourselves an idol in the form of anything in heaven above or on the earth beneath, or water below."

(Deuteronomy 7:25, 26) "Neither shall you bring an abomination (idol) into your house."

Examples of modern idols:

- Crucifix (pain and suffering)
- Mother Mary (Mother of Jesus)
- Pictures and paintings of Jesus
- Buddha statues - any religious or false gods
- Blessed or devoted thing – candles, incense
- Evil devoted thing (Joshua 7:17-19)
- Curious arts and artifacts (Acts 19:19) – amulets, good luck charms, *Nefertiti* necklaces.

The following are true examples of accursed objects in the lives of Christians, how their lives were affected, and how they were delivered.

Amulet can be defined as, "something worn by someone, either on the wrist or neck for protection from evil." Once while I was praying for the sick and casting out devils, a woman who had severe shoulder pain came to the altar for prayer. It was so painful and stiff that she could not lift it over her head without suffering terrible pain. I prayed for her several times, each time having her try to raise her arm above her head, and each time she failed to do so because of the pain. Not knowing anything else to do, I began to pray in tongues, seeking the Lord's wisdom. As I continued praying, the Holy Spirit directed my eyes to the amulet she was wearing around her neck. It was made of two shades of leather, which was wrapped around something, and was attached to a leather neck-

136

lace that hung around her neck.

As I stared at it, I knew in my heart that it had something to do with the pain she was experiencing. So I asked her three questions: What did it represent? Where did it come from? How long had she worn it? She told me that it came from Africa. I believe that she bought it in a boutique and wore it for a couple of months. I found out the pain in her shoulder didn't start until she started wearing the amulet!

I informed her that it was cursed and was causing her pain. If she took it off, she would be healed. She agreed and as soon as it was removed we prayed again. This time I led her through a prayer to break the curse, renounce the demon of pain, and I cast it out of her shoulder. The pain left immediately, and she was once again able to raise her arm above her head without any restriction or pain! I instructed her to never wear the amulet again. I also encouraged her to pray over her whole house and trust the Lord to reveal any other objects that might be cursed, and remove them.

Note: Be careful of objects that you pick up in foreign countries and items you purchase in boutique shops. Many times, these objects have been cursed by witches and warlocks. They have been chanted over and certain demons of sickness, disease, divorce, poverty, and so on, have attached themselves to these objects. Wherever these objects are allowed to stay, they will inevitably be visited by whatever demon the curse carries.

Trolls at the Bed and Breakfast — A *troll* is, *a supernatural being (demon); a giant or dwarf, living in a cave.*

Several years ago, I decided to take a well needed weekend break from the ministry. After searching the telephone book and making several calls, I found a nice quiet Bed and Breakfast where I could spend two days and nights in peace.

Immediately after checking in, I was shown to my quarters. I was tired so I lay down and began reading my Bible. The room was full of sweet smelling *PlugIns®*. I could hardly breathe. I got out of bed to unplug them, but in the process, I observed a little wooden statue made from the stump of a small tree. Positioned on top of the stump was an ugly little face of a man with evil eyes and a sorcerer's hat on its head. It had long scraggly hair, was very ugly and evil looking. It is what some people call a troll.

My immediate thought was, "I'm out of here!" I went back to bed to talk to the Lord about the situation, thinking I had come to the wrong place. But the Lord told me I couldn't leave, so I lay back down again. The Lord further revealed to me that there was another troll in the room. So I once again, got out of bed and went to the other side of the chest of drawers, and there I saw the other one. It was much like the first one, except it looked even more scraggly and old. Arguing with the Lord that I wanted to leave, I went back to bed and lay down. A few moments, later, I saw a little gray demon come out from the little statue and walk over to my bed, climb up and hover over my head! This time I pleaded with God to let me go, asking Him what was going on, and once again He said to me "No! I sent you here to minister to these people. I won't let it (demon) hurt you."

The Holy Spirit began to reveal to me that there were actually three of these trolls in the house, all sent to bring curses. He said that I was not to worry, only to be at peace and rest.

I submitted myself to God's care, thanked Him, and drifted off to sleep, quietly resting without any further incident. But when I woke up the next morning, my left arm was folded across my chest over the other shoulder and I couldn't move it! Not only could I not move it, but my hand felt numb and looked a little deformed. I thought, "Jesus, you said you wouldn't allow this thing to hurt me."

As quickly as I had this thought, I began to say the name of Jesus repeatedly within myself until the temporary paralysis left and I was able to move my arm and fingers. I felt the Lord was undoubtedly letting me know, without a doubt, that these demons were sent to destroy the family.

I began praying in tongues, the Lord responded by revealing the following to me:

1. These people were not going to make any money because one of these trolls was a demon of **poverty.** (Their Bed and Breakfast had been opened for about a year, but business had been very slow).

2. A spirit of **infirmity**, represented by the second troll, was causing the husband's sickness. The Lord revealed to me this man had been suffering diabetes for nine years and his condition gradually worsened over the last three years. He suffered numbness, poor circulation and pain. The Lord also revealed that the same spirit of infirmity had attacked someone else who had slept in the room I occupied, with rheumatoid arthritis!

After these things were shown to me, the Holy Spirit instructed me to call the husband and wife to my room to share all this information with them. When they called me for breakfast, I declined and asked to speak with them. I told them everything I had experienced and all that the Lord told me. Donna, the co-owner, affirmed everything the Lord revealed:

1. They had struggled with the business for no apparent reason.

2. Her husband, Jeff had indeed been sick for nine years and the last three had been worse!

3. Her mother had also slept in the room I was renting and had suffered with rheumatoid arthritis until she died!

I then asked her where the third troll was. She said there weren't anymore. I assured her that I heard God clearly say that there were three. After thinking for a moment she remembered that there was one in the other room under the coffee table. This one was smaller than the other two, just as ugly, only one thing was different – he was cross-eyed. The Holy Spirit told me that the third one was a spirit of **confusion** and was attacking them all, especially their son, Dave, who had a problem staying in one place. He had been back and forth between Michigan and Florida. He seemed to be double-minded and couldn't secure or hold on to a job.

I explained witchcraft, curses, and how one can allow entry of demons into their house from bringing cursed objects in. Then, I told them that in order to have peace, health and prosperity, they would have to burn the accursed things. At first Donna resisted, because she thought they were cute and she bought them while on vacation in northern Michigan. But after I explained the consequences to her (more sickness, poverty, and so on), she conceded. I then led her and Jeff to recommit their lives to the Lord Jesus and prayed for their business and their health. I had gone there for one purpose but God had other plans for my stay. He wanted to set in order, a house of three precious people and bring His peace. I didn't rest much, but I left there with great joy.

It is important to periodically inspect and cleanse your home of objects that may be associated with curses. Sometimes other family members bring in objects such as the following:

- "Cute little" dolls
- Angel figurines
- Buddhist objects
- "Blessed" candles
- Excessive accumulation of animal objects like leopards, owls, elephants, snakes, and so on.
- "Blessed" (cursed) incense (that attracts demon spirits when lit)
- Magazines
- Books

- Pictures of Christ or Mary
- Pictures that manifest anger or fear
- Native American charms such as dream catchers or objects from other cultures that have been enchanted to bring forth fertility, and so on.

Word Curses

Proverbs18:21 states, "Death and life are in the power of the tongue and those who love it will eat its fruit." A word curse is a curse or disabling state of being brought on by evil and corrupt speaking, either casually or purposely. When a person speaks words that are contrary to the Word of God, and bring about vexation of soul, debilitating situations, confusion and harm, demonic spirits are released to carry out the evil spoken.

(James 3:6-10) [6] "And the tongue is a fire, a world of iniquity: so is the tongue among our members, that it defiles the whole body, and sets on fire the course of nature; and it is set on fire of hell. [7]For every kind of beasts, and of birds, and of serpents, and of things in the sea, is tamed, and hath been tamed of mankind: [8] But the tongue can no man tame; it is an unruly evil, full of deadly poison. [9] Therewith bless we God, even the Father; and there with curse we men, which are made after the similitude of God. [10]Out of the same mouth proceeds blessing and cursing. My brethren, these things ought not so to be." So then the course of nature (life) is set on fire (vexed, hindered, destroyed) by hell. Proverbs 6:2 says, "You are snared by the words of your mouth. You are taken by the words of your mouth."

The following should be considered concerning word curses:
- Evil words that others have spoken against you. If you are walking in righteousness, they cannot affect

you. However, if someone speaks divination and you receive their words, it *will* affect you.

- Evil words that we've spoken against ourselves can open a door for the enemy to come in.
- Evil words that we've spoken against others (law of sowing and reaping).

Curses From The Womb

When words are released into the atmosphere they are either empowered by the Holy Spirit or by the devil. The Bible tells us that we will give an account of every idle word we speak (Matthew 12:36). As stated above, words can either bring life and health or sickness and death. A positive word inspired of God can bless a person immensely. On the contrary, a curse spoken over someone can affect them negatively for the rest of their lives, even from the womb. Such is my own testimony.

Although my life with my wife was very blessed, there were times throughout our marriage that I would find myself very disgruntled and irritable with her. We could never have a disagreement without me defending myself, retreating to my room, or feeling frustrated. I would also get these feelings when debating or trying to prove a point with other women. Over the years, I was never able to articulate these feelings nor associate them with any definite moment or situation like I do now. So, the years continued to go by as my wife and I experienced these frustrating episodes with no explanation.

Then several years ago while praying with a friend, it was revealed to her that there was a **spirit of meanness for women** in me. I knew enough about her to know that she heard clearly from God, and I could trust her discernment. Plus, even as she spoke those words, I had a flashback of tense moments with women, in which I saw myself raising my hand to strike them. This never really happened, but in those moments I would get a quick image of myself striking them. Of course I would resist the urge, but it would always leave me a little disconcerted.

So, realizing that she was correct, I cried out to the Lord to reveal to me when this "thing" entered into me. The Lord didn't say anything, but in the next instance I saw the name of my dead grandmother spelled out on the screen of my mind. Upon seeing her name, there was an overwhelming flood of pain that followed. All at once, I felt tremendous hurt, pain and rejection that came from the depths of my soul and I realized that she had hated me. I knew she had been the midwife who delivered me at birth. I also knew that she wanted me to die in my mother's womb, and had uttered it, either at the time of delivery or during the weeks and months leading up to my birth.

At that moment I felt the pain of death. The pain was so intense that tears flooded my eyes, and I doubled over, crying out as that rejected infant in the womb long ago, "Lord, she hated me! She wanted me to die, Lord! She wanted me to die! I hate her!" These words came out of my mouth in the voice of an infant! In that moment, I was that unborn baby sixty years ago.

After a moment of intense sobbing, I knew that in order to be delivered and healed I had to forgive her. I spoke the words out of my mouth, "I forgive her Lord, and I forgive her, in Jesus' name!" Immediately, after speaking those words of forgiveness, I renounced the devil and it came out of me, screaming as he left.

The next day was Sunday, and I found myself crying all day, at church and at home. I realized that I was going through inner healing. After sixty years of unexplained pain and hurt, I was finally being healed and restored. Though I was crying outside, inwardly I was experiencing a joy and freedom I never had before. There was now a greater sense of love and acceptance for women. God had set me free.

Later on as I meditated on events preceding this moment, I remembered my mother telling me that my paternal grandmother did not like her. Neither did she believe that I was my father's child. Because of her intense hatred for my mother, it is easy to understand how she could speak word curses about me. Whether she spoke them ignorantly or deliberately doesn't matter, the effect was the same. In speaking words of death such as, "I hate her. This is not my son's child. I hope it dies," she released demons of death, rejection, and meanness for women into me through my mother's womb. These spirits affected my life for sixty years, causing great pain, broken relations and discord in my marriage. I thank the Lord for His great love and faithfulness in revealing this truth to me so that I could be set free. It has helped me to help others and I hope it will help you.

Now let's focus on what happened to me. My deliverance came about through the following steps:

1. Through prayer and intercession, it was revealed to me that there was a **spirit of meanness for women** inside of me (which interfered with my relationship with my wife and others).
2. Realizing it was true, I sought the Lord for understanding on how it entered me.
3. The Holy Spirit revealed that my grandmother had cursed me in my mother's womb through hateful words.
4. I then realized that I had hatred in my heart for her.
5. With the help of the Holy Spirit I forgave her (forgiveness is absolutely necessary when one has been offended or hurt).
6. I renounced and cast out a spirit of meanness, rejection and death.
7. The following day the Lord began the process of inner healing, which lasted all day.

Curse Broken In the Womb

Once while discussing the topic of witchcraft with a friend named June, I shared the story of another young lady whose baby was born retarded. At this time, the child was about four years old when I first visited the mother. The Holy Spirit gave me a word of knowledge that the baby had been cursed in the womb. I asked the mother if she ever visited a "reader" (another word for a fortune teller or witch) while pregnant with her son. She replied, "Yes."

I asked her if this "reader" had spoken words over her baby, because it was possible that the fortune teller had spoken curse words over her child. She immediately told me this woman had not only spoken words over her, but had literally declared that the baby would be born retarded! As a result a demon of retardation had entered the child in the womb! I encouraged her to get involved with a church and commit her life to Christ, and that the Lord would deliver her child. Although the truth was revealed to her, I could do nothing for the child because the woman would not get into a church to be strengthened so that change could occur.

As I continued to talk, I noticed that June, who was pregnant, was looking strained and hurt. Suddenly, she asked me if I would pray for her and her unborn child. She said that her husband had been joking around regularly, saying that the unborn child was going to be retarded. She told him to stop, but he would only laugh and continue to do it. She asked me could her husband curse their unborn child by calling the baby retarded. I told her that if we didn't pray, it could happen. She asked me to talk to him because when he would speak the word "retarded", she would feel strange.

I consented to talk to him when the opportunity presented itself, but first I wanted to pray for her baby. I first asked her to forgive her husband, and then I had her place her hand on her stomach and renounce the *spirit of retardation*. I placed my hand over her hand and com-

145

manded the spirit to come out of the baby. Immediately, June began to cough as several demons began to come out of her. These spirits were coming out of her baby through her mouth! Praise God! I didn't call out any other specific demons (I simply commanded Satan to loose her and go). But because the manifestations and coughing were so strong I believe many others came out of her, including rejection, death, and retardation.

After casting the devil out of June and her unborn baby, I asked the Lord to touch the baby from the top of its head to the tip of its toes. I prayed for the baby's mind and every organ in the child's body to be healthy. God faithfully answered our prayer because the baby came into the world beautiful and healthy, with a sound mind. Praise God!

Authority Engendered Curses

Authority engendered curses are those brought on or allowed by the spiritual neglect or unrighteous rules of those in authority.

Authority is the power or right to command, act or influence; the power that comes with responsibility to watch over and protect someone or a group, as parents are to children.

God has given parents the right and the power to raise, nurture and protect the children He has given them.

The following Scriptures reveal that all authority comes from God:

(Proverbs 8:14-16) [14] "Counsel is mine, and sound wisdom: I am understanding; I have strength. [15] "By me king's reign, and princes decree justice. [16] "By me princes rule, and nobles, even all the judges of the earth."

As Christian parents, we are to keep our children safe from satanic influence and entrapment. If we stand in righteousness, God's angels will protect us and our family. If we disregard the commandments of God to walk in holiness and resist evil, we will open the door for the enemy to attack our heritage.

Some years ago, I had the opportunity to experience such a situation. Through the sins of the mother her child was attacked by the devil. This lady was an insurance client of mine who I serviced once a month. She was a single parent with one little boy whose age was about a year and a half. He was a playful boy and would greet me every month with a big smile and climb up on my knee. He had big beautiful eyes and was a delightful child. His mother was a very nice Christian woman. However, there was one problem; she was having an adulterous affair with a married man.

I also learned that she was an "out-of-fellowship" Christian. When the opportunity presented itself, I talked with her about the ramifications of adultery and fornication. I explained that because she was a single parent and the head of her household, she was responsible for the spiritual welfare of her son. I further informed her that if she didn't repent and stop fornicating, her son would possibly be attacked in some way by the devil. She listened to me, but continued the adulterous relationship, disregarding my warning.

After about a month, I visited her house again and saw her son looking very peculiar. His eyes were glossy and listless and he was drooling at the mouth. Instead of the bright-eyed, happy little boy I had seen before, the child was now looking like he was suddenly retarded. I asked Joyce what was wrong with the boy. She vehemently replied. "I don't know! I woke up one morning and he was like this. I hate him!"

"Hate him?" I asked. "Joyce, this happened to this child because you refused to get out of this illicit relationship. If you will repent and stop seeing this man, God will heal your son", I told her.

This time Joyce conceded and asked me to show her what to do. I then led her in a prayer to seek God's forgiveness for her sin, renounce her relationship with the man, and renew her covenant with the Lord. With her permission, I then placed my hand on the boy's head and commanded the demon of retardation to, "loose the boy and go." There was no immediate sign that he had been delivered, but when I returned a month later, I was greeted with a pleasant surprise.

When I entered the house, I was embraced by the bright-eyed little fellow I was accustomed to seeing! I asked Joyce what happened. She informed me that one morning, three days after I prayed for him, he climbed into her bed just as bright-eyed and happy as before. She was elated that her son was normal again. So was I. She went on to tell me that she immediately broke ties with her "lover" and returned to church. I left there that morning praising the Lord and thanking Him for His goodness.

What happened? Let's consider some things. Although this woman brought a curse upon her son through her sin, God provided a way of deliverance through the blood of Christ. How?

1. She repented (had a change of mind and heart).
2. She asked for forgiveness.
3. She broke ties with her partner in sin.
4. We broke the power of the curse and cast the devil out of her son.
5. Her house was back in divine order and she returned to fellowshiping with the saints.

Curses released through perverted preaching

A particular pastor, because of his anger and lust, began to preach out of anger and frustration and defiled many. Not only did he release anger into the congregation but suspicion as well. People started to distrust one other and petty competitiveness mounted, causing dissension in the Body. People became apprehensive about bringing new people to the church for fear they would be ridiculed and driven out.

After a while, his preaching took a turn for the worse. He began to lace his messages with lustful remarks and insinuations. It became so evident and so alarming that he was approached by other leaders in the church and admonished to stop or he was going to lose people. Rather than heed the advice, he grew worse.

One morning while preaching, the sexual remarks became so graphic that it became repulsive. Suddenly, the Holy Spirit spoke to one of the leaders and told him at that moment, the pastor released lust spirits upon the congregation. In the ensuing weeks and months, things changed dramatically. Fornication broke out in the congregation and pregnancies began popping up alarmingly! Many people were perplexed and didn't understand what was happening. Apparently, the Word of God had been taught to these young people and they were supposed to know better. But what happened?

An ordained man of God has the authority and power to do one of two things: he can release the life-changing power of the Holy Spirit through his anointed preaching, or he can, through perverted preaching, release spirits of darkness upon the people that bring shame. This particular pastor did the unthinkable; he ignorantly released unclean spirits upon God's people.

We as ministers and leaders must be careful of not only what we teach, but *how* we teach. For the Scriptures state that teachers shall receive a stricter judgment. "For we all stumble in many things. If anyone does not stumble in word, he is a perfect man, able also to bridle the whole body" (James 3:1,2).

Note: Today, in 2004, it is a known fact that little girls between the sixth and eighth grades are being sodomized at an alarming rate, and are performing oral sex on at least eight-to-ten boys per week. Could it be that one of America's ex-Presidents — who was proven guilty of performing a certain sex act in the White House — by his implication that oral sex is not real sex; added to the perception that such acts are acceptable?

Could it be because of the promiscuity and perversion of our top leader, that increased curses of lust were released upon this nation? If we judge by Scripture, we will have to say, "Yes" (Prov. 14:34; Prov. 29:2).

Witchcraft Curses
Witchcraft curses are evil, supernatural power over people and their affairs through wicked practices such as incantations, potions, spells, artifacts, and so forth.
These types of curses are released through incantations (words that engage demonic powers) that puts one in league with demons, allowing them to attack, control, and harass people, and even make them sick and die. Examples: fortune telling, tarot cards, ouija board, divination, sorcery, and so on.

(Ezekiel 13:17-19) [17]"Likewise, son of man, set your face against the daughters of your people, who prophesy out of their own heart; prophesy against them, [18]and say, "Thus says the Lord GOD: "Woe to the women who sew magic charms on their sleeves and make veils for the heads of people of every height to hunt souls! Will you hunt the souls of My people, and keep yourselves alive? [19]And will you profane Me among My people for handfuls of barley and for pieces of bread, killing people who should not die, and keeping people alive who should not live, by your lying to My people who listen to lies?"

In this passage it describes false prophetesses who confused their own ideas with the Lord's. They cast magic death spells on people by working sorcery or witchcraft through use of charms and veils.

People who have delved deeply into witchcraft by cursing people and using demons to sexually seduce people will experience violent deliverance. The demons are given entrance through several ways: either by an individual joining himself to them by a vow or he has been used to unwittingly speak spells upon others.

Contemporary Example of Witchcraft

There was a situation in which a young man was married to a woman whose father was from Jamaica. This father hated his son-in-law so much that he worked witchcraft in order to end the marriage. In order to do this, he sent an Indian doll to his daughter from Jamaica that he had possibly cursed by incantations. He probably confessed that wherever the doll was placed, it would bring rebellion, strife and divorce.

One day, the couple's little boy remarked that he didn't like the doll because it made strange faces. While visiting this family, the young man told me about the strange occurrences of this doll. So, I observed it for myself. As I stared at it for a short while, to my amazement the doll's face literally changed expressions. The look it gave me was one of disdain and it looked as though it was challenging me. I immediately realized that it was witchcraft and its purpose was to divide this family.

The young man asked his wife to discard the doll but she refused to part with it. Instead, she hid the doll from him. As time went on, she became increasingly rebellious, hateful and violent, eventually committing adultery.

Although this was a Christian family and generational curses of divorce had been broken over them, she chose to accept the whispers from the demon of divorce that had been released through the doll. The demonic spirit was whispering to her such things as, "You don't love him", "You don't need him", "Don't you remember how he hurt you?" "You deserve someone better, so divorce him."

Despite the fact that the young man prayed to God and fought to keep their marriage together, she adamantly resisted his attempts to save it and consequently, the marriage dissolved.

What happened in this situation? You may be thinking, "I thought curses didn't work on Christians." Usually, witchcraft doesn't affect a Christian if he or she is walking in obedience to God.

In this case, because of this woman's **refusal** to **submit to righteousness and obey the commands of God** and her husband, she succumbed to the suggestions of the enemy. Her disobedience and rebellion allowed Satan to use her to commit adultery and leave her family. God cannot protect you from witchcraft if you choose to give your members over to it. In order for God's protective power to work in our lives, we must cooperate with the Holy Spirit, by submitting to righteousness and adamantly resisting Satan's promptings.

For the weapons of our warfare are not carnal but mighty in God for pulling down strongholds, casting down arguments and every high thing that exalts itself against the knowledge of God, bringing every thought into captivity to the obedience of Christ (2 Corinthians 10:4-5).

When Satan tries to lead us away from God with rebellion and sin, we must steadfastly resist him. His suggestions will come through thoughts (imaginations) dreams (images). Whether sleep or awake, the moment we realize our mind is being bombarded with evil thoughts, we must immediately rebuke the thought or dream and cast it down. We must train our spirits to wake up immediately from sleep and cast down the images (lust, violence, vengeance, and so forth). Here's how it is done:

1. When the thought comes, cast it down by opening your mouth and commanding the thought to go: "I rebuke this evil thought, I don't receive it and I command this image to go, in Jesus' name!" Command the devil to go by saying, "Devil, I command you to take your wickedness and go away, in Jesus' name!"
2. If the enemy puts a lustful, sad, hopeless or demonic song in your mind, cast it down by doing the following:

   • Command it to go by saying, "I rebuke this song. I command it to go in Jesus' name!"
   • Play a Christian gospel, praise or worship CD/tape to fill your mind with praise. If you don't have a tape present, ask God to give you a song. He will stir up your spirit and bring a song of praise to you.

Note: We as Christians should fill our days and evenings with praise, worship and the Word of God. When we do this, we keep our minds stable and train our spirits to always be alert to demonic attacks.

Steps to Breaking Curses
1. **Affirm your relationship with the Lord Jesus:**
   "Lord Jesus, I believe you are the Son of God; you left your throne in heaven and became a man. You lived in this world and were in all points tempted as we are, yet without sin (Hebrews 4:15). *You defeated Satan on the cross, when you rose from the dead and ascended. I belong to you. You are my Savior, my Lord, and my Deliverer"* (Revelation 12: 11; 12:17).
2. **Repent of all sins, known and unknown:**
   "Heavenly Father, I come to you with a repentant heart. Please forgive me of all my sins, the ones I

am aware of and those I'm not. I am sorry for them all."

3. **Renounce the sins of your forefathers:**
   "I confess the sins of my forefathers. I now renounce, break and loose myself and my family from every ancestral curse of all demonic bondages placed upon us because of sins, transgressions and iniquities through my parents and forefathers."

4. **Repent of any involvement in the occult or false religion:** *"Father, I ask your forgiveness for involving myself in the occult, a cult, or any false religion."*

5. **Renounce occultic spirits and demons of curse:** Command them to come out in Jesus' name. Be specific and name the particular demon of curse. For example, lust, incarceration, idolatry, insanity, and so forth.

CHAPTER THIRTEEN

Transference of Spirits

To *transfer:* "To carry or send; to reassign or convey. 1 Corinthians 15:33 states that, "...evil company corrupts good habits." Another truth says, "Association breeds assimilation." These truths bring to mind two thoughts:

1. **Demons influence the mind**
2. **Demons infiltrate the body**

The mind is influenced when one associates with evil people who communicate evil, such as doubt, unbelief, fear, lust, hatred, anger, and so on. That person will inevitably take on the same belief system, along with their thoughts and attitudes. These negative thoughts will set up mindsets that will be conducive to demonic manipulation of that person.

For example, if a Christian hangs around worldly people who swear and curse, such thoughts will both infect the mind and eventually cause this person to swear and curse also. If one associates with lustful, hateful and angry people, this individual's soul will eventually be filled with lust, hate and anger. This person has been contaminated with worldly thinking because of wrong associations.

But there is something deeper and more insidious than just thinking worldly. Demons not only influence the mind but they also infiltrate the body. How is this accomplished? We know that if a person thinks a certain way, he will inevitably act on what he thinks. But these actions are not his alone. What has happened? The word *assimilate* means, *to absorb and incorporate*, which further means, *to merge with someone or something in thought or in deed (to become one)*. The inference is, like a sponge that soaks up whatever liquid it touches, so will a person, if unguarded, absorb whatever is in the atmosphere. Likewise, the intentions of demons are to contaminate human beings by infiltrating their bodies. Sometimes demons are also sent to infiltrate people's homes, jobs, and so on. This is accomplished through the air or the atmosphere and through people they have entered who become carriers.

To *carry* implies two things: (1) the demons are carried inside the contaminated person's body or (2) there is an entourage of demons following the contaminated person around, that will enter unsuspecting persons who are ignorantly associating with the contaminated person. If a person fraternizes with homosexuals, even without establishing a relationship, he will receive a demon of homosexuality into his body. Likewise, if one associates with fornicators, liars, thieves and haters, that person will assimilate demons of lying, thieving, hatred, and any others that come with them.

The following are examples of how demons can be transferred:

- **By watching television or movies** that contain lustful scenes, violence, murder, horror, and so on. When a person attends a movie and watches these types of scenes, the soul and body is open to the infiltration of evil spirits.
- **By association with wicked people**, especially during the teen years and early twenties. Young men and women can be infiltrated by alcoholic spirits, drugs, lust, witchcraft, because of the pres-

sure to conform to the subculture in which they live.

- **By the laying on of hands,** our Lord Jesus instituted the doctrine of laying on of hands as a means of transferring the anointing of healing, deliverance and the impartation of spiritual gifts.

   When Elijah was taken up in the whirlwind, Elisha received the double portion of Elijah's spirit when his garment fell on him. Likewise, when a person places his or her hand on another individual, there can be an impartation of whatever spirit(s) is coming from the person who is laying hands. If there is a spirit of anger in a person who has been angry or disgruntled with a spouse before coming to service, and is still unrepentant, and then lays hands on someone, that same spirit of anger will be transferred. The unsuspecting saint can leave the service angry, sad, or irritated, never knowing the reason why.

Note: I believe that leaders should teach their elders and ministers to never come to service angry or distraught. Always maintain a pure heart of love and walk in forgiveness.

- **Through sex acts** (This would include unlawful kissing). When two people kiss, not only are they connected physically, but there is a bonding of souls and transference of demonic spirits. During the sex act, many spirits can be transferred to an unsuspecting partner. Whatever is in one individual will enter the other (fears of all sorts, rage, perversion, confusion), because the Scripture states in 1 Corinthians 6:16, "that he that is joined to a harlot is one body with her."

Note: Single Christians should not pet or fondle or kiss each other. Kissing is only to be done between married couples. Kissing is a prelude to sexual intercourse. The purpose is to arouse one's sexual appetite. Paul said, "It is better to marry than to burn" (1 Corinthians 7:9b).

Sexual Lust in Baby

A friend of mine shared a situation with me that makes it clear that demons are no respecter of persons. While visiting a friend, this minister was fondled by his friend's little three-year-old girl. The baby walked over to him and touched his private part. Jumping back startled, he immediately informed the mother that her child needed deliverance.

With her consent, he commanded the devil to loose the child, at which time the baby fell on the floor and began writhing like a snake and making sexual movements. After taking the child through further deliverance he was instructed by the Holy Spirit to tell her what had happened to the child.

Because she and the baby's father were not married and were living in a sinful state, they had opened the door to satanic attack upon their child. They had been fornicating around the baby and spirits of lust, fornication and perversion had entered the child. Through their sins, lust and perversion had been transferred to their daughter.

This dear lady, who was a Christian, repented and changed her lifestyle and her baby remained free.

The following example reveals how demons can enter a person through course jesting (vulgar jokes).

Demon of Jesting

By associating with carnal people and participating in course, vulgar joking, a particular Christian woman was attacked by unclean spirits. This lady was with family and friends, fellowshiping and having fun, when suddenly the conversation changed to telling jokes.

Someone told a vulgar joke about fornication and everyone started laughing, including this Christian lady. As she began to laugh, something came over her and she couldn't stop laughing. She laughed so uncontrollably, that she fainted.

During a class, in which I was teaching on the subject of transference of spirits, she shared her story, and asked, "Why did I pass out? Did something come into me and make me faint?" Rather than directly answer her question, the Holy Spirit directed me to have her raise her hands and repent of participating in course jesting. After she asked for God's forgiveness, I had her renounce the spirit of jesting, rebellion and fornication, and commanded the devils "Out!" At that point deliverance broke out. She doubled over and began to cough involuntarily, as other spirits came out of her, including a spirit of death. She was amazed! Her countenance immediately brightened.

By the leading of the Holy Spirit, I explained to her and the class, that when she laughed at the unclean joke, she opened herself up to the invasion of unclean spirits, who came into her with such force they made her faint. God was merciful and gracious allowing her to learn an invaluable lesson: **Be ye separate and come out from among them** (2 Corinthians 6:17). Although as Christians, we would like to make others feel comfortable in our presence, we still cannot compromise our righteousness. We must please God.

(Ephesians 4:22-24) "That you put off, concerning your former conduct, the old man which grows corrupt according to the deceitful lusts. And be renewed in the spirit of your mind, and put on the new man who was created according to God, in true righteousness and holiness."

CHAPTER FOURTEEN

Healing Of Demonic Sicknesses Through Deliverance

"How God anointed Jesus of Nazareth with the Holy Spirit and with power who went about **doing good** and **healing** all who were oppressed by the devil. For God was with him" (Acts 10:38).

This Scripture is an indication that in God's eyes, healing and deliverance are one and the same anointing. The word *saved* in Romans 10:9-10, is the Greek word *sozo*, meaning *healed, cured, delivered, and restored*. This salvation is for the total man — spirit, soul and body (Isaiah 53:4-5). The spirit of man is *saved* by the regenerational power of the Holy Spirit; the *soul* or mind of man is renewed or changed by the study, revelation and application of God's Word; and the body is healed (mended), salvaged and restored through the power of healing and deliverance from satanic oppression.

All sickness is not caused by a demon, but much of it is. And when there is sickness involving demons, a person cannot be healed or hold on to the healing without the demon being cast out. Cases in point:

The word *healed* is used by the Holy Spirit in describing the **deliverance** of several women and Mary Magdalene from evil spirits in Luke 8:1-2: "Now it came to pass, afterward, that He went through every city and village, preaching and bringing the glad tidings of the kingdom of God. And the twelve were with Him, and certain women who had been *healed* of evil spirits and infirmities—Mary called Magdalene, out of whom had come seven demons,"

The classic example of deliverance from sicknesses and infirmities caused by a demon is found in Luke 13:10-16. There was a woman bowed over for eighteen years by a *spirit of infirmity*. The fact that he is called a **spirit** of infirmity indicates his evil work was to cause weakness in the woman's body to the extent that she literally was bowed over and couldn't straighten up. The demon's *job* was to keep her bent over by constant pressure on her spine, head and neck for eighteen years! But along comes Jesus the Messiah — and what does He do? In verse 12, He cries out and says, "Woman, you are loosed from your infirmity," at which moment the demon leaves her. He is cast out by the power of Jesus' word.

But the woman, though free of the demon, is still bent over! Again, what does Jesus do? Verse 13 states, "And He laid His hands on her and immediately she was made straight and glorified God."

In order for the woman to be totally healed, first the demon of infirmity had to be cast out so she could receive her healing. Once the source of her infirmity was gone, Jesus could then release healing power in her body in order to lubricate her discs, or dissolve any calcium build-up in her vertebrae, and strengthen her weakened back and stomach muscles so she could straighten up.

It is my belief that many times the reason people don't receive their healing is because the spirit of infirmity is still lodged there. Although they initially receive their healing, whenever the pain returns, their faith is tested and they lose hope that they were ever healed. Therefore, the spirit of infirmity must be cast out.

Thoughts to consider:

In this passage of Scripture, this lady was not born with this disease or infirmity, because she had it for eighteen years before Jesus set her free. Which means the demon of infirmity could have come into her under one of several conditions:

1. She had an accident by falling, slipping, and so on.
2. She cursed someone and cursed herself.
3. Someone cursed her or cursed herself by continued unrepentent sin.

Conditions under which this could happen:
   a. Being around the wrong people
   b. Sins of ancestors left the door open
   c. Ignorance of the power of her own tongue in speaking against leadership, herself or others
   d. Unforgiveness and bitterness in her heart
   e. Disobedience to God's commands

How was Jesus able to discern that there was a demon involved? By the anointing of the Holy Spirit, Jesus had supernatural insight (John 5:30) into the situation. By the manifestation of the gift of discerning of spirits and/or the word of knowledge, (see Chapter 8, *Necessary Strategy of the Holy Spirit*) He saw and knew the demon was there. 1 Corinthians 12:7 states, "But the manifestation of the Spirit is given to each one for the profit of all."

Today, the Holy Spirit wants to anoint you, the believer, to do the same works that Jesus did. Mark 16:17-18 says: [17] "And these signs will follow those who believe: In My name they will cast out demons; they will speak with new tongues; [18]they will take up serpents; and if they drink anything deadly, it will by no means hurt them; they will lay hands on the sick, and they will recover."

As a believer, you **can** also cast out devils and heal the sick. Repeat the following confession daily to build your faith:

I am a believer and these signs do follow me. In the name of Jesus, I cast out devils. I speak with new tongues, I take up serpents and if I drink any deadly thing, it shall not harm me. I lay hands on the sick and they do recover.

The following are several accounts and personal testimonies of how God used me in dealing with spirits of infirmity to bring healing. I am sharing this not to bring attention to myself or my office, but rather to encourage you, the believer, that God is no respecter of persons. He will use anyone who avails himself to be used. As a matter of fact, at the time this particular incident happened, I was not known as a prophet, but an insurance agent, going about my business of writing insurance and collecting premiums.

Case #1
This dear lady was a client of mine who I visited once every month to collect her insurance premium. At that time, she was a Muslim, worshiping Allah. I had been witnessing to her periodically about Jesus, the Son of God, and how in His name only, could one find salvation. During one of my visits, I found her holding her stomach and moaning in pain. I asked her what was wrong, to which she replied, "I haven't had a bowel movement in over two weeks!" I found out she had taken one laxative after another to no effect. I was impressed to pray. So I asked her could I pray for her. She consented.

I took her by her hands and began to pray in tongues, when suddenly I **saw** into her body by the Spirit, and observed a demon with hands as big as baseball gloves. He was squeezing her intestines so they wouldn't move. I immediately commanded him, in the name of Jesus, to let her go and he went out of her, at which point she breathed a sigh of relief. The look on her face was one of astonishment.

Her next statement was, "Lee, I felt like there was a steel band around my waist, but now it is gone." I asked her, "Whose name did I use? Who set you free? Allah, or Jesus?" She replied, "Jesus!" I was then able to lead her into receiving Him as her Savior. I prayed for her stomach and intestines asking God to regulate her bowels. This same lady today is a prophetess and being used by the Lord Jesus.

John 5:1-15 tells of a man healed (delivered) at the Pool of Bethesda. In this passage of Scripture, we find a man at the Pool of Bethesda who had been paralyzed or infirmed for thirty-eight years. After questioning the man of his desire to be healed, Jesus commands him to "Rise, take up your bed, and walk!" Immediately he was healed, walked, and glorified God. Later on in verse fourteen, Jesus instructs the man: "See, you have been made well. Sin no more, lest a worse thing come upon you."

This statement indicates that something worse — a greater sickness, stronger demonic force — would come into him if he opened the door by either continuing in sin or returning to a previous sin.

Jesus indicated in Matthew 12:43-45, that when a demon is gone out of a man, he seeks rest, finds none, and finds seven other spirits more wicked than himself, and they all enter the man and live there, bringing far more destruction and mental torment than before. This can only happen if a person goes back to disobedience and sinful living, thereby frustrating the grace of God.

As was the case with the woman in Luke 13, we find the same situation with this man:

1. He was not born with this paralysis because Jesus *knew* that he had been in that condition a long time (thirty-eight years).

2. "Sin no more, lest something **worse** come upon you," indicates he was an active sinner before this demon attacked him. He could have been a fornicator, delved in witchcraft, cursed others, laughed at sick people, blasphemed, touched God's anointed, and so on. It could have come upon him suddenly, gradually, or by an accident.

Personal Experience

The following is an account of my personal experience with a person who after being healed, refused to obey God, and had something **worse** come upon her.

While conducting insurance business with this particular lady, I learned that she had a back problem. She had fallen in a store where she worked several months before, and was suffering great back pain while walking, standing or sitting. During our conversation she shared with me that she had filed a lawsuit against the store. I asked her if I could pray for her. She said I could.

I laid my hands on her back, rebuked the devil and released healing into her back. The pain immediately left her. She was amazed. She could now bend over and walk without pain. We rejoiced for a few moments, and then the Lord Jesus instructed me to tell her that in order to keep her healing, she must drop the lawsuit against the store because there was no reason and no need for money or doctors. She had received God's *best*.

She refused to drop it. She wanted the money. In order to get the money, she would have to *lie*, and say she was still disabled, denying the power of God and giving Him no glory for what He had done. After pleading with her awhile, I finally left. She was perfectly well.

Over the course of several years, I watched her deteriorate, until she finally had to get around in a wheel chair.

She refused to obey God. She lost her health and never received any money. Something *worse* came upon her — total paralysis, poverty, and eventually death.

Forgiveness

Forgiveness is a necessary act in order to receive healing and deliverance. We are reminded by the following Scriptures, that God is not only grieved by our unforgiving heart, but because of our disobedience, He is forced to turn us over to evil tormenting spirits. Satan hates us but God loves us, and has given us not only a way to keep from falling, but a way to be delivered if we do fall. That way is forgiveness:

"And do not grieve the Holy Spirit of God, by whom you were sealed for the day of redemption... and be kind one to another, tenderhearted, *forgiving* one another, even as God in Christ forgave you" (Ephesians 4:30,32).

"And his master was angry, and delivered him to the torturers until he should pay all that was due to him. So my heavenly Father also will do to you if each of you, from his heart, does not *forgive* his brother his trespasses" (Matthew 18:34,35).

But what is forgiveness? *To forgive is to give up resentment against someone and the desire to punish; to forgive is to pardon and to require no retribution.*

According to Matthew 18:1-35, to forgive is to give up one's right to be angry; to show mercy; to give up hatred and spitefulness; to write off a debt owed; to pardon and forget because we have been pardoned by God, the King.

Forgiveness is an act of faith to release someone from a debt by the power of God's grace (ability). Forgiveness is a response to God's love for us... "For God so loved the world that He gave His only begotten son" as a sacrifice for us. It is also a command of God and our responsibility (Mark 11:25).

Results of Unforgiveness
When we refuse to forgive, we open ourselves up to the tormentors of fear, doubt, bitterness, anger, sickness, instability, insanity, foolishness and death (Matthew 18:34).

If we choose to hold anger or hatred in our hearts, we separate ourselves from the favor and peace of our Lord. The Word tells us "But if you do not forgive, neither will your father in heaven forgive your trespasses" (Mark.11:26).

Rewards of Forgiveness
It is only by grace through faith that we are able to pardon someone who has sinned against us. We are empowered by the Holy Spirit to have the courage to release a person. It is our trust in Jesus that He will not allow us to come up short, but will compensate us with His provision of love, peace and restoration that reinforces our resolve to forgive.

After one has dutifully fulfilled God's requirement of forgiveness, he will then drink of the fruits of righteousness (Matthew 5:6).

What are the fruits of righteousness?
- Agape love
- Grace (favor)
- Supernatural peace (calm)
- Rest
- Supernatural joy, which is the strength of God.

Love is the impetus for faith, and covers a multitude of sins against us. It wards off a besetting spirit of retaliation. A habitually attacking spirit comes to relentlessly harass, to the extent that one constantly thinks of venge-

ful acts. Perfect love casts out the fear of not gaining resti-
tution so that thoughts of vengeance find no place. So
when we walk in perfect love, fear does not exist.

Grace, which is the favor of God, is given to us in our
obedience to forgive. When we choose to obey God, it not
only gives us favor with God, but with man also by opening
up doors of opportunity that would otherwise be closed.
Found in this favor is also health, prosperity and restored
relationships.

Supernatural peace or stillness defies the effects of negative circumstances. This peace is full of light that darkness cannot overcome, understand or resist. It is filled with
the faith of God because we are trusting in God's Word:
"Be still and know that I am God." He **will** fight off the
devourer for our sake.

The rest of God is quietness and serenity which produces
stability in our thoughts and emotions. God has promised
that when we obey Him, He will give us rest from our enemies (fear, anxiety, anger, confusion and stress).

Joy is the supernatural, childlike, ecstatic laughter in the
face of adversity. It passes all understanding and is foolish
to the carnal mind. Holy laughter, a product of joy, is supernaturally imparted at the moment of one's obedience to
giving, forgiving, and so forth. Demons cannot understand love, joy or stillness. It brings total confusion to them.

When we decide to forgive, we set off a chain reaction
of forgiveness in ourselves and our offender that denies
the entrance of a spirit of vengeance. When we act in love,
the peace of God surrounds us, penetrates our soul, qui-
ets our emotions and brings rest within our body. Now,
we experience God's calming, reassuring and comforting
presence. We have supernatural confidence. For example,

"A soft answer turns away wrath, but a harsh word stirs up anger" (Proverbs 15:1). The soft answer disarms the demon of vengeance or hatred in the other person.

Forgiveness must be practiced on a daily and even on a moment by moment basis. There must be consistency. (Matthew 18:21-22) "Then Peter came to Him and said, "Lord how often shall my brother sin against me, and I forgive him? Up to seven times?" Jesus said to him, "I do not say to you, up to seven times, but up to seventy times seven."

The Act of Forgiveness

I used to think that forgiving was equated to saying, "I'm sorry" or apologizing to someone, or them saying the same thing to me. But God taught me that forgiveness is an act of your will and has to be spoken through your mouth from your heart. If one is mute due to a physical impairment, then it should be spoken by one's spirit. When you are forgiving, it is not necessary to go to someone and tell them, "I forgive you." This is pride. The offender doesn't have to know that you are forgiving them. If possible, it would be good for him to know that he or she has offended you. But, the offender's knowledge of his offense, doesn't guarantee that he will apologize or even acknowledge his wrong. When one forgives another, the act is between *the offended* and God. If I have been offended, the most important thing for me to do is please God. Pleasing God is obeying His Word, which commands us to forgive. (Mark 11:25). Therefore, I do it out of love for God, knowing He has forgiven me and will reward my obedience.

How It Is Done

Father, I have been hurt by _____ and I am angry. I realize that you forgave me for Christ's sake (Ephesians 4:36) and accepted me in the beloved. So I choose today to forgive my brother or sister. _____ I forgive you and I release you in Jesus' name. I pray God's richest blessing on your life. I decree that salvation and deliverance be released to you in Jesus' name.

Now, Father, please forgive me for holding animosity in my heart against my brother or sister. I receive your forgiveness and I thank you in Jesus' name.

I believe that this woman's heart, in Luke 13:10-16, had been dealt with by God, before Jesus called her over to himself. I believe she was already repentant and had surrendered her heart to God and had cried out for deliverance. Subsequently, the Holy Spirit led the Lord Jesus to her to show His mercy and compassion.

Deliverances Through Repentance and Forgiveness:

Headache healed

I once visited a lady who was suffering with a terrible headache. As we carried on the conversation I could see she was in great pain. So I asked could I pray with her. As I began to pray the Lord revealed to me that she was in a state of unforgiveness. How? I sometimes sense it in my spirit, and at other times I see the word spelled out *unforgiveness*. I asked her if she needed to forgive someone, and if anyone had hurt her? At first she said, "No." Then she remembered that she had just gotten off the telephone with a neighbor who had upset her and she was still angry.

I then explained to her the reason for the headache. She was angry and distraught and needed to forgive her neighbor. I told her that if she would forgive from heart she would be healed. She consented and I led her through a prayer to forgive her offender, and then we asked the Lord to forgive her. As soon as we finished praying the headache left her. She learned a valuable lesson that day — that when you hold animosity in your heart for someone it can make you sick. But when you forgive, God will heal and deliver you from demonic oppression.

Repentance is a weapon against Satan. It is also a form of submitting to God and resisting the devil. The result is he will flee.

Note: Sometimes, the headache, stomachache, and so forth, will simply go away after prayer. But, at other times you may have to do as Jesus did — command the spirit (headache infirmity) to "GO" or "COME OUT!"

Women with crippling back pain healed

Case #2

Ann was a lady who lived next door to a believer's house, in which we held Bible study every week. She had been in and out of the hospital for chronic back pain. But instead of getting better, it grew worse, to the point she could no longer walk. She had continued to lose weight until she looked anorexic. It was as if something was sucking the life out of her. One night, someone asked if I would pray for her. I suggested that the whole Bible class go over to her house. When we entered her bedroom she was a pitiful sight. We immediately began to pray in the Spirit (tongues) seeking God's guidance. The Lord told me to talk with her about her spiritual life, her relationship with the Lord. I found that she believed in Jesus, but was living in a state of sin, committing fornication. I wasn't sure of her salvation, so I led her through a prayer of repentance, expressing godly sorrow for her sins, and asking the Lord to forgive her.

We broke the power of that spirit of infirmity and commanded it to come out of her body. She was still in pain, so we turned her over on her stomach and to our surprise we could see through her gown an image in her back. Her lower body was covered by the blanket so I had one of the ladies pull her gown up so we could see clearer. What we saw was astonishing. It was the image of a demon! It was very dark and about four inches in length. It had a body like a tyrannosaurus rex dinosaur. It had a long mouth

172

like an ant eater and appeared to be sucking the life out of her back.

We continued to command the demon and the pain to come out of her back. She was still groaning in pain. By the leading of the Holy Spirit, I instructed the ladies to lay hands on her back, and we all did warfare in tongues. In the midst of this, I heard the enemy speaking subliminally, saying if I didn't stop he was going to attack my daughter. I rebuked him and continued to pray. (Demons will try to frighten you into ending the warfare by threatening to harm someone you love.)

In obedience to the Holy Spirit we continued praying, and after about ten or fifteen minutes we began to see progress. The image in her back was starting to fade away!

As the image faded the pain progressively subsided. After about forty minutes the pain had totally left her and so did the demon of pain and paralysis. We looked for the image and it was also gone.

At this point this dear lady sat up in the bed thanking us. We told her to give God the glory. She looked one-hundred percent better, and was now able to walk. Before we left, she received the Holy Spirit and spoke in unknown tongues.

What were the steps in this precious lady's deliverance?

- We prayed in the Spirit seeking God's will. Praying in tongues is speaking secrets to God. He talks back and reveals secrets you need to know.
- We followed the Lord's directions in what to do (how to war).
- I talked to her about her spiritual condition.
- I led her into repentance (she asked for God's forgiveness).
- We broke the power of that infirm spirit in her life.

- We commanded Satan to leave.
- We laid hands on her and prayed until the image and pain left.

Note: Although there are certain guidelines for casting out and healing the sick, we must remember that it is not by our might (ingenuity) or power but strictly by the Holy Spirit. He is the strategizer. No two deliverances are the same. We must depend totally on Him.

Case #3

Elaine was a woman who suffered with chronic, excruciating back pain. She had gone through a series of deliverances, but she couldn't keep her freedom, because of recurring bouts with a spirit of unforgiveness. I had prayed for her on several occasions and she had experienced a degree of relief from the pain, but inevitably the pain would return.

But as I continued to minister to her over the ensuing months, I noticed some problems in her character. I found out that she was very critical of people and she never could really forgive her ex-husband for the things he had done to her. She also had unforgiveness for her ex-pastor, the church, her daughter and son-in-law. She had attended the healing school for several years, and had been taught the power of forgiveness, but couldn't walk in it. So, after talking and counseling with her on several occasions, she decided to come to class for deliverance. It turned out to be one of the most beautiful deliverances I had ever seen.

The time it took to set her free was approximately an hour and a half. As the deliverance session began to unfold, the Lord would deal with each person she hated, the situations surrounding the painful incident, how they had hurt her and her subsequent anger and bitterness. The battle was at times very intense and time consuming. At times the memory of certain incidents would be so fresh and the sorrow so deep that she would moan and groan, holding her stomach and doubling over.

Along with the sorrow and grief, there was deep-seated anger and rage toward her ex-husband, her daughter and son-in-law. She felt betrayed and rejected by her husband who had committed adultery on her and turned her daughter against her. More recently her daughter and son-in-law had rejected her, believing she was insane and the cause of the divorce.

This hurt her deeply and she developed a tremendous resentment for them. As I tried to lead her through prayers to forgive each one, a battle would ensue. She would vacillate from anger to sorrow, sometimes arguing that no one understood how much she was hurting, and that she had a right to be angry. When I finally brought her to a place where she was willing to forgive I would have to bind the demons who were keeping her tongue from saying "I forgive". I would command the spirit to shut up and loose her tongue, and then call her name and encourage her to use her will and forgive.

This went on for over an hour. But every time she would forgive and renounce the different spirits of anger (each demon would be associated with a different person) there would be a degree of deliverance. There would be coughing and screaming and yelling and moaning. We would talk, we would pray. She would forgive and she would seek forgiveness. She would renounce and we would cast out.

We continued this way until every spirit left her. I had her stand to her feet and laid hands on her back and prayed. She continued to grimace from the pain that was still in her lower back. I asked the Lord what was wrong. He didn't prompt me to cast out anymore demons, but told me to have her speak to the pain and repeatedly say, **"I am healed. The pain is gone!"** We continued this for about five minutes until finally the pain totally left her. She was demon free and pain free. A spirit of unforgiveness and bitterness had a stronghold on her life. Once the unforgiveness was broken and bitterness cast out the pain in her back could be healed.

Lady Healed of Arthritis

A neighbor once asked me to pray for her because she had suddenly developed severe arthritic pain in her knee. She had been having little episodes of pain, but the pain became so severe that it adversely affected her job performance. As I headed towards her home I prayed in the Spirit and asked the Lord to show me how to minister to her. I was impressed with the thought of forgiveness — that whatever previously occurred in her life resulting in pain, invoked a need for her to forgive.

As I began talking to her, I asked if anyone had broken her heart or seriously hurt her emotionally. She told me that her husband had hurt her about twenty years ago. At that time, he hit the lottery and received a large sum of money and ultimately, ran away with her best friend. She was left to raise the children alone. As time went by, she grew very bitter. Her heart was filled with hurt, anger and hatred. Over the years, the bitterness had taken a toll on her mind and body. A spirit of infirmity had set up residence in her knee, eating away at the bone and cartilage, causing excruciating pain.

I informed Ms. Mathis that in order for her to be healed, she would have to repent of her bitterness and hatred. She also needed to forgive her husband and the woman for their sin against her. She agreed. We prayed seeking God's forgiveness for her years of hatred and bitterness. Then she verbally forgave her husband for his infidelity, deception, hurt, anger, hatred and bitterness. We both commanded them to "come out in Jesus' name." After she was delivered from bitterness, she was now able to be delivered from the spirit of arthritis. We commanded him to come out of her knee and ministered healing to her by the laying on of hands. She was instantly set free from the pain and all damage to her knee healed.

CHAPTER FIFTEEN

Ministering To Children

Ministering deliverance to children is similar to that of adults, yet there are a few slight differences. From the following, we explore the similarities and differences.

Similarities
Children have a spirit, a soul, and a body just like adults. They can be hurt, disillusioned, confused or demonized just as grown-ups. As a matter of fact, demons enter people in their childhood. Most of our problems with rejection, fear, anger, and so on, can be traced to our childhood. The extent of demonization, oppression and influence, depends on the circumstances in which a child lives and the amount of demonic activity around him or her. Children, like adults, can have varying degrees of demonic influence; thus, some cases may require greater warfare.

Differences
In most cases, children are much easier to be delivered than adults. Why? For two reasons: 1) They haven't been exposed as long and/or haven't operated in willful sin as adults have; 2) Whatever spirits may have entered their soul, have not been there very long. Their stronghold on the child's psyche is not as great.

The following are the most common mindsets and demons that one has to deal with in children:
- Rejection
- Fear
- Hurt
- Anger
- Rebellion
- Disobedience
- Procrastination
- Varying degrees of violence, retaliation, lust (depending on circumstances and environment).

The warfare will be greater or lesser, depending on the following:
- Age category, whether the child is an infant, a toddler, a small child, or an adolescent.
- Depth of the child's sin and rebellion.

Infancy (birth to one-year-old) — An infant's will isn't yet developed because he or she hasn't willfully and repeatedly sinned.

Toddler stage (two-to-three years old) — The same as infancy: The child is not able to understand willful sinning.

Childhood (from four or five years of age to eleven or twelve) — A child's will is developing and is weak but he or she is able to make conscious decisions. (The level of innocence will vary according to knowledge and maturity).

Puberty — Anywhere from age 11-13 (The beginning of sexual reproduction).

Adolescence — From puberty and into young adulthood. Legally, parents have authority over their children and to a certain age, over demon spirits that would attack them.

During infancy to about age five, where warfare is concerned, parents can cast the devil out of their child. However, once the child develops their will and willfully sins, if he or she wants to be delivered, they must exercise their will to be set free. They must seek forgiveness from God and forgive others.

The following are actual examples of what one may encounter and how to pray for children.

1. If a child is one-to-five-years old, a parent can lay hands on the child and cast out a spirit. If the parent is unequipped in warfare, the minister may cast the devil out with the permission of the parent. The reason is that the parent(s) have authority over the child — the minister does not.

2. Somewhere around the age of six or seven, or whenever he can understand, a child must be taught to forgive. This may vary according to maturity level. In some cases, five-year-olds may be mature enough. When applicable, somewhere during the deliverance sessions, because of offenses, the child **must** exercise his or her will in forgiving and seeking forgiveness like every other believer. Because these children are able to use their wills in choosing to sin (although they are manipulated by Satan), they must also use their will to forgive and seek forgiveness. Then once they forgive and renounce the spirits, they can then exercise their will to be set free.

3. A five-year-old child or younger may not be able to understand forgiveness, and in these cases, God will allow the authority of the parent to bring forth deliverance. As stated before, infants can be offended and experience hurt and anger thus receiving spirits of rejection, anger, violence or rebellion. If these spirits are not cast out, they will abide in the child and his or her rebellion and violence

179

will grow stronger as they mature into puberty and young adulthood.

4. A young adult must be treated and dealt with as you would an adult.

Many times I have had to minister to young adolescents, who are angry with a parent, a teacher, a friend, and so on. These young people have to forgive and seek God's forgiveness before the Lord can deliver them.

In the case of a parent offending a child, the parent(s) must humble themselves and ask the child to forgive them. This satisfies the commandment in Matthew 5:23-24:

23 "Therefore, if you bring your gift to the altar, and there remember that your brother has something against you, 24leave your gift there before the altar, and go your way. First be reconciled to your brother, and then come and offer your gift."

The following are actual cases that may help you understand how to minister deliverance to children.

Case #1

One of the students in my school had a small one-year-old child that repeatedly scratched and beat her. One night, she brought the child up for prayer and deliverance. I proceeded to command the spirits out to no avail. The child squirmed and whined, trying to break away. I asked the Holy Spirit what was wrong. He said, "She (the mother) yells and screams at him. His spirit is offended. Have her ask him to forgive her."

I turned to her and asked, "Do you yell and scream at him?" She replied with tears in her eyes, "Yes, but I don't want to keep spanking him. I don't know what to do."

Note: You cannot spank a demon out. You will only bruise the child, physically and mentally.

When I instructed her to ask the child's forgiveness, she was astonished. But I assured her that if she did, the demons would then leave the baby. She complied and then asked the baby to forgive her. I commanded the demons of anger and fighting to leave him and after two or three quick sighs, he reached for his mom, his eyes now bright and receptive to his mom. Once she asked for forgiveness, the devils had no hold on the baby. The child was now free to enjoy his mother's love.

Case #2

The grandmother of a little girl, five or six years old, called me to pray for her granddaughter. She was having a terrible time trying to wash the child's hair. The child would get extremely frightened, hysterical, and violent. The little girl would have no problem taking a bath, but if you came near her head, there was a fight.

When I got to her house, we prayed in the Spirit, seeking God's wisdom. What the Lord revealed was that the child was afraid of drowning. Water on her head, eyes closed, and so on, caused her to panic for fear of drowning. Once the spirit was revealed, I had the grandmother place her hand on her grandbaby's head and take authority over the spirit of fear of drowning. She gave me the permission (authority) to cast it out, and I did. The child coughed slightly and was set totally free. From that point, there was no problem getting her hair washed.

Wounded spirit

What is a wounded spirit? When we speak of spirit, we mean both the innermost being of a child and the soul. A wound comes from continued situations of rejection with no explanation or refuge for a battered soul. There is a frequent bombardment of pain and anguish to the point where a child sees no reprieve from hurts received. When a significant other like a mother or father, continually rejects a child by refusing to affirm him, that child loses confidence in himself because his relationship with his parents is uncertain. Much needed love and acceptance is denied. Therefore, emotions run up and down because certain secrets may be revealed or the child is embarrassed in front of people feeling betrayed causing his self-esteem to be shattered or lost. This person's trust in a parent, a friend or even God can be destroyed.

This is how a child feels when the spirit is wounded: *One day I'm accepted, the next day I'm berated and talked down to. I continue in a state of flux (constant ups and downs), never knowing what to do to maintain my father's, mother's or teacher's approval. The child goes on an emotional roller coaster — from fear of disapproval, hurt, fear of rejection, embarrassment, anger and resentment — to false joy. Questions arise frequently: "Am I going to be rejected today (yelled at, berated)? Should I laugh now, or remain stone-faced? What do I do to win his/her approval? What do I do to keep from being yelled at? What does it take to win his/her love and approval?"*

This cycle of disapproval can cause manic depression which is a serious mental health problem involving extreme swings of mood (highs and lows). It is also known as Bipolar Affective Disorder.

A child must learn to forgive and put his or her trust in another significant one: either a trustworthy family member, counselor, pastor or friend. Many times a good youth pastor can save a young person from self-destructing.

A spirit can be defined as, the character or disposition of a specified nature in a person; a mental disposition characterized by firmness or assertiveness or lack of assertiveness.

Possible spirits that are taken in by a child with a wounded spirit — fear of rejection, self-rejection, rejection, self-disdain, self-abuse, nervousness, confusion, anger, hatred, rebellion and murder.

Can these spirits produce a serial killer who is constantly killing the gender of the person (mother) who rejected him? Or, could he possibly be killing the gender of the one (father, or mother's boyfriend) whom he perceives caused his significant other (mother) to reject him? If you discern that a child's behaviors reflect the manifestation of the above mentioned spirits, then please minister to him by doing the following:

1. First, you need to have the individual sit down and counsel with him or her from the Word of God.
2. Teach them the benefits of forgiveness.
3. If the offender (parent, guardian, and so on) is present, then whenever possible, encourage them to seek the child's forgiveness. Have the parent admit to the child that he or she is sorry for having hurt them.
4. Lead the child through forgiveness (repentance) and have him forgive his offenders, renounce the demons and cast them out.
5. There will be a need for follow-up ministry to ensure that the child doesn't have a relapse. The parents must be determined to give the child an environment of love and support.

CHAPTER SIXTEEN

Ministering To Victims of Abuse

Since this book's primary focus is healing and deliverance, it is necessary to explain the root cause of the demonic manifestations that destroy people's lives. Manifestations such as sicknesses, diseases, and mental disorders, stem from the following attitudes and emotions:

- Rejection
- Hurt
- Anger
- Resentment
- Bitterness
- Hatred
- Fear

The most common one is fear which will be explained later.

Rejection

Rejection is a precursor to all demonic manipulations and strongholds of fear, hurt, guilt and shame. These are a few of the emotions that are evoked by physical, verbal and sexual attacks from others. All of these emotions can lead to more violent emotions such as anger, rage, fighting, murder, and so on. Where healing and deliverance is concerned, the deliverance minister will always have to deal with the *spirit of rejection*. Rejection always precedes the emotion of hurt and anger. Where there is anger, there is hurt and hurt comes from rejection.

Rejection can be defined as, *repudiation, denial and dismissal*. This means that the rejected person is made to feel worthless, discarded, unwanted and unloved. This is a form of death and can wreak havoc on a person's self esteem. Rejection can cause a person to become introverted, withdrawn, and disassociated with people. This person may never find fulfillment in any relationship, because he never feels loved. Because of this person's fear of being rejected, he may be invaded by *spirits of rejection, fear of rejection, and self-rejection*. Because of the tremendous need to be loved, a person can be driven to look for love in the wrong places. This person can become relentless in his or her pursuit of love and intimacy to the point that he or she receives a spirit of whoredom, going from one lover to another, never finding fulfillment. Abortion can result due to unwanted pregnancies and divorce.

On the other hand, rejection can cause a person to become very angry, critical and abusive. The first moments of rejection can begin in early childhood. It can even come from the womb, when a mother or father voices their opposition to the child being born. The child (fetus) can sense or even hear the parent(s)' disapproval of it living. A spirit of rejection may enter into the child in the womb. Later in life, spirits of rejection can enter by a teacher disregarding the person by giving more praise and attention to others in the class. A friend, relative or lover may reject the person in the same way (preferring someone else over him or her), causing great hurt and pain. Many times, these feelings of hurt cause a person to rebel out of anger. He may become very bitter, critical and hurtful to not only friends, but those of his family.

Hurt

Hurt is an emotion that follows the feeling of rejection. When one feels rejected, it is like being stabbed in the stomach or heart. It is a dagger that penetrates the soul and tears open the heart of an individual causing them to recoil in pain.

The word *hurt* is defined as *injury or wound; ill treatment or punishment.* A person can be hurt many times in life but unless he knows how to forgive, he will walk around in agony all his life. Hurt can come from being called an ugly name or from deception and infidelity by a spouse. The pain of divorce, the experience of being fired from a job, racial prejudice, sexual harassment, and job discrimination can cause deep hurt. When such attacks of hurt occur and the power of forgiveness is not exercised, spirits of hurt will enter and torment the person with a dull ache in the heart. Hurt will always lead to anger. Many times when casting out spirits of rejection you will have to also cast out a spirit(s) of hurt. A *spirit of hurt* is what makes a person feel the physically, empty ache in the heart (located between the chest and stomach).

Anger

Anger is a natural result of one being hurt by someone. But the Bible tells us to "be angry and do not sin." (Ephesians 4:26). This probably sounds kind of strange to some of us, because we feel it is impossible not to be angry when someone hurts us. But how is it a sin? The Word of God tells us to avoid the natural progression of anger, which leads to sin. In the second part of this verse it says, "Do not let the sun go down on your *wrath.*"

The definition of *anger* is, *a feeling of displeasure or hostility that a person has because of being injured, mistreated or opposed.* But the meaning of *wrath* is much stronger. It is *an attitude of intense anger, rage and fury.* Wrath borders on madness and vengeance. This type of anger is very destructive, involving hatred and murder.

When a person has moved to such a state of mind as this, he has sinned and must repent and seek God's forgiveness. Why? Because he has opened himself up to demonic invasion. If one does not forgive shortly after the offense (hurt) and the initial feeling of anger, he will meditate on the offense and his hostility will grow until he is invaded by *spirits of anger and rage*. Whenever deliverance does take place, the minister may have to cast out several demons of anger because of the different offenses.

Resentment

When a person resents someone, he or she feels or shows displeasure, hurt or indignation for that person. It is a dislike for the offender and being in that person's presence brings irritability. A *spirit of resentment's* purpose is to destroy relationships and can lead a person to become moody, critical and obstinate (very disagreeable).

Bitterness

One of the most common doors of entry for demons to work in the life of a person is through bitterness. Hebrews 12:15 says that we should look carefully "Lest anyone fall short of the grace of God; lest any root of bitterness springing up cause trouble, and by this many become defiled." When a person becomes bitter, he or she can defile many by the sharpness of the tongue. This person can not only be critical and abrasive, but contrary and rude! A bitter person is very hurtful and can never be satisfied, because the *spirit of bitterness* that is operating in the person can never be appeased.

The purpose of the spirit of bitterness, is to keep reminding someone of all the hurtful incidents of his or her life. Because these memories are kept alive like they happened yesterday, the person constantly meditates on the hurts and the people who hurt him. People who live under the influence of these spirits suffer with a variety of mental and physical problems: confusion, melancholy, depression, insanity and fears of all kind. Bitterness will cause people to suffer from physical diseases such as cancer, arthritis (rheumatoid), kidney problems, blindness, migraine headaches, and so forth.

When you minister to a person suffering from bitterness you can expect to cast out such spirits as: unforgiveness (keeps alive every detail of the hurts, no matter how trivial), bitterness, resentment, hatred, murder, arthritis, death, and so on. The list can go on and on. The key is to be led by the Holy Spirit.

Hatred

The Word of God states, in 1 John 3:15, "Whoever hates his brother is a murderer." Hatred is such an intense emotion of disdain and hostility toward a person that God equates it with murder. As a matter of fact, these two spirits along with rebellion operate together. One, who is in the throes of hatred, unconsciously plots evil in his mind toward his brother.

So, during the deliverance session, the minister will have to cast out *spirits of hatred* (sometimes for each offender), *murder, anger, vengeance*, and so forth.

Fear

The Word of God tells us that "God has not given us a spirit of fear, but of power, of love and of a sound mind" (2 Timothy 1:7). The work of a *spirit of fear* is extremely wicked in that it can totally debilitate a child of God. It can rob him of his faith in God, in himself and in others. Satan knows that in order to please God, a person must exercise faith in the promises of God. Without faith, it is impossible to go anywhere, not only in God, but in life, period! Fear directly opposes a person's faith and trust in the Lord.

The Scripture above reveals the enemies intent: to rob us of the stability of a sound mind, and rational clear thinking (the ability to make intelligent decisions). When one is operating in fear, he has no trust in the power of God. Therefore, he feels powerless to perform the simplest tasks. This person may have such spirits as: *fear of man, fear of being embarrassed, rejected, molested, raped or left alone.* These spirits can make people afraid to go outside, drive a car or walk across the street.

One of my friends is a Vietnam army veteran who fought and killed to survive. He was a rough and tough fighting machine. It didn't seem that he feared anything. But today, he is afraid to drive a car! Why? Because a *spirit of fear of losing control of the car* kills his faith in himself and God. When dealing with spirits of fear, remember if there is one present, there are also more, because they run in packs. Depend on the Holy Spirit to help root them out.

Grief and Sorrow

When ministering to victims of abuse who have suffered the loss of a loved one or experienced divorce, you will always have to deal with spirits of grief and sorrow. The meaning of grief and sorrow are about the same. A person suffering from grief and sorrow can be full of remorse and despondency. Overall, there are feelings of being alone and death. A death, divorce or the separation from a dear friend, can leave a big hole in a person's heart. Sometimes one is left depleted of drive and energy. In other cases, some people seem to recover relatively quickly. But I believe everyone needs help during such a crisis.

God allows us a normal time of grieving: It varies according to the circumstances. Sometimes it can take anywhere from six weeks to a year. But even during this time, if a person suffers from guilt or feelings of abandonment, the process can take even longer. With proper Christian counseling, love and support from family, a person's healing should progress very well. But if after a normal time of grieving, a person is still crying, showing signs of regret and bouts with depression; or if the person is still regressing and separating from people, becoming more remorseful and sad, more than likely, he or she has received *spirits of grief and sorrow.*

The emotions generated, can range from guilt, to fear, to anger and rage. Largely, this is according to the type of relationship a person experienced, how it ended, and the circumstances surrounding the death or divorce. In most cases, the candidate will need deliverance from spirits of grief, sorrow, fear of being alone, abandonment, anxiety and even anger and bitterness. This is not always the case. As always, through counseling and the leading of the Holy Spirit, coupled with divine patience, one can help bring healing to a hurting soul.

How to deliver a person from grief and sorrow
1. Have the person pray to the Father and ask him to deliver him/her from grief and sorrow.
2. If necessary, ask the person to forgive the individual who has died and left him, or the spouse that has divorced him/her.
3. Tell the candidate to ask God to forgive him for holding animosity in his heart for the deceased, and so on.
4. Lead the candidate in a prayer to release the person into God's hands.
5. Renounce the spirits of grief, sorrow, depression, loneliness, and command them to come out, in Jesus' name.

Prayer of release from grief and sorrow
Father, I forgive my mother (loved one or spouse) for dying (divorcing) and leaving me alone. Please forgive me for any anger or animosity I have harbored in my heart against them or you. I refuse to blame You. _____, I release you to God. I let you go. Lord, take my loved one

and I give him or her, to You. I release _____
(spouse) and I sever all ties with _____.

*Spirit of grief and sorrow, and so forth. I renounce you
and command you to come out of me, in Jesus' name. Amen!*

Incest, Molestation and Rape

When a person has been raped or molested during childhood or even as an adult, many times the questions arise, "Where was Jesus, and why didn't God protect me?" The person(s) perceives that God either hated him or didn't care about him. They feel rejected and betrayed by God, who is "Almighty" and can do *anything*. Many times deliverance cannot come until the issue of *blaming* God is dealt with. In a case like this, the person's heart is filled with rejection, self-rejection, self blame, anger and fear of the opposite sex, anger toward God, bitterness and low self-esteem. There can be a tremendous identity crisis. The only person that he should identify with, the only one (Jesus) that can help him, becomes the object of their hate and distrust. He is bound by lies — "God doesn't love me and He won't help me."

How do you free a person from the lie? Truth! The Word of God says, "You shall know the truth and the truth shall make you free"(John 8:32). The only way to combat a lie is to replace it with the truth. We must share the truth with the candidate.

Truth: Strong's (1659) Greek: eleutheroo — *To make free – remove liability; to remove one's disadvantage; one is no longer subject to the lie.*

To be made free means one no longer has to respond to the lie; the lie loses its power to persuade and manipulate one's emotions and will. We are no longer taken captive at the *devil's* (liar's) will.

How do you heal an embittered person?

At first the truth may not seem fair; may not satisfy

one's desire to *get even,* nor immediately remove the sorrow or grief. It may hurt at first, but will eventually make one free. How? Once a person finds out the real truth – that is, the one who is really to blame for their pain and misfortune, and why certain things happened to them, only then, can they direct their anger in the right direction (at the devil and those he used to perpetrate the evil), and subsequently seek God for help. Let's look at what lies, misconceptions and truths must be considered.

LIE: *God doesn't love me.*
TRUTH: God is all good, can do no evil, nor tempt with evil. (James 1:13). God is love.

LIE: *God hurt me.*
TRUTH: Satan is the perpetrator of all wickedness, hates all humans; he is the father of lies, who comes to kill, steal and destroy. Jesus came to bring abundant life.

LIE: *I don't understand how that could happen to me. I'm a mistake.*
TRUTH: Curses — generational (incest, transgressions of law), personal sins, word curses, and so on. The person must understand how curses come down to affect the third and fourth generations. Curses can go back as far as ten generations. Explain that many things happen to us because of a familiar spirit that is sent to *work* the curse in the family. You will probably have to discuss the laws governing curses, and so forth.

LIE: *Why did God let this happen to me?*
TRUTH: Since God can do no evil, we must understand that God may have been trying to caution the family members (mother, dad, and so on) to stop or take note of the atrocity, but because of their sins and preoccupation with other things and even participation, he was unable to get their attention. Explain to the individual that because

he (the victim) survived it, God sustained their life and preserved him to be able to one day deliver someone else who has the same or similar experience. "Because they survived, they can revive." Their place of pain will be their place of reign.

LIE: *No one else has suffered like me.*
TRUTH: The curse is broken (Galatians 3:13, Hebrews 8:35). Jesus suffered for all of us, taking our sins and penalties upon Himself on the cross that we may be free.

LIE: It's impossible for me to be healed. I'm too bad.
TRUTH: God is the healer. He sent Jesus (the Word) to heal us. He is able and willing to heal us of every emotional and physical pain (sickness) we have incurred to the point that we will no longer remember the pain; neither experience the torment of sorrow and grief. He is able to restore us completely (Hebrews 4:16).

Once these truths are received, the person is then ready to forgive, receive forgiveness, place the blame where it belongs, release the Lord, renounce the devil, cast him out and go through the process of inner (emotional) healing.

NOTE: An individual, who has suffered rejection (molestation, rape, abuse, and so on, and has been delivered, can understand a person who is suffering from rejection and abuse better than anyone else. This person will have great compassion for others who are hurting. The anointing will be great upon such a man or woman. He who is forgiven for much will love much.

Judy – Religiously bound to spirits of infirmity and death.

Judy is an ordained minister who loves Jesus with all her heart, but suffered from many ailments: arthritis, diabetes, heart palpitations. She also received a kidney transplant. One night as I was ministering healing by the word of knowledge, she came forward to be healed of arthritis and pain in her back. As I prayed for her, I sensed a spirit of death and infirmity. I attempted to cast it out of her but to no avail. There was no real deliverance that took place. So as I prayed, the Holy Spirit revealed that she had been molested as a child. When I first began to question Judy, she denied such a thing ever happened to her. But then, the Holy Spirit gave me specific ages and dates when the molestation took place. She finally admitted that it was her father who had done it to her! Up to this point she had been ashamed to admit it.

The Lord revealed that Judy was angry with God, her mother and her dad. She was angry with her dad because he had taken advantage of her, angry with her mother because she never did anything to help her, and angry with God because He *allowed* it to happen to her.

Before any real deliverance could take place, I had to lovingly convince her that God never deserted her, but loved her through it all. I explained to Judy that He was now ready to set her free from all the hurt, anger, bitterness and infirmities that had broken down her body. She came to understand that she had to forgive her dad, her mother and stop blaming God.

It wasn't fair to Judy or her husband to remain in that state of melancholy. With the ups and downs of depression, her joy was being stolen and so was her husband's. She had a religious spirit which allowed her to perform *church work* and a limited life of fellowship while she was dying within. I informed Judy that God was ready to deliver her and use her mightily in setting others free who were experiencing the same afflictions she had suffered.

Finally, Judy agreed to forgive everyone, including God, and let them go. Once she was led through prayers of forgiveness, and renunciation of demons of rejection, self-rejection, anger and bitterness, she began to be delivered. Something broke in the Spirit. Demons of guilt, shame, hatred, murder, and fear also came out of her. The curse of death was broken over her and I released healing into her body to remove arthritis, diabetes, and heart palpatations. God did a wonderful work that night! There was a beautiful glow on her face and in her eyes — warmth that had not been there before. When I last saw Judy and her husband, they were happy and doing well in ministry.

Steps to build self-esteem
1. When you fall (fail, sin) get up and dust yourself off. God is not promoting your sin, but He does love you (Romans 8:32) and understands the reason for your inconsistency.
2. Come to God, don't run away (Hebrews 4:16). God has provided a mercy seat through Jesus. His mercies are renewed every day. Ask God to forgive you.
3. No matter how many times you fail and fall back into a sin, know that God is always ready to forgive you (1 John 1:9). If He expects us to walk in perpetual forgiveness (Matthew 18:21-22), how much more will He forgive us? Perpetually! He requires nothing of us that He is not willing to do Himself.
4. Forgive yourself and don't down-talk yourself. Forgiving yourself means letting yourself off the hook. If God has released you from your debt, why would you offend Him and insult Him as a parent by holding yourself in chains of self-guilt, self-rejection and self-abuse? If we do self-penance, we insult the work Jesus did on the cross. If we inflict punishment on ourselves to prove we are sorry, we do damage to God's creation (our body), which is a sin (1 Corinthians 3:17 and 1 Corinthians 6:19). Forgiving yourself allows you to once again hear

the voice of God and walk in confidence and fellowship with Him (1 John 1:7).

5. Continue to acknowledge (speak) who you are in Christ Jesus, identifying with who He says you are (Philippians 1:6).

6. Seek out and stay around people who will love you and build you up emotionally (a strong Christian, support group). "Not forsaking the assembling of ourselves (yourselves) together..." (Hebrews 10:25).

7. Develop a good relationship with the Holy Spirit, learning His word, staying in a church of strong faith, worship, and training for Christian work.

8. Prayerfully, find rewarding Christian work – work that will not only bless other people, but help you feel good about your worth.

9. Take planned steps to change your thoughts and patterns of perfectionism, self-rejection, self-defeating talk and criticism of other people.

10. Practice love thoughts, speech, activity, accepting yourself and accepting their faults as well as your own, and believing for the best in every person. This is the love walk. Love yourself. Love your neighbor. Love God.

Daily confessions to build up your self-esteem

1. I will not judge others, lest I be judged (John 6:37).

2. Love dwells in me; I am love, therefore I am not puffed up or self-centered (1 Corinthians 13).

3. I believe the best for my brother or sister (1Corinthians 13:7). Therefore, I will not detract from them but I support and highly esteem them.

4. I am God's workmanship, created unto good works (Ephesians 2:10).

5. I am accepted in the beloved (Ephesians 1:6).

6. I am fearfully and wonderfully made (Psalm139:14).

7. God has not given me a spirit of fear but of love,

power and a sound mind (1 Timothy 1:7).

8. When I am hurt and mistreated, by the power of God, I can forgive and love again. When I am ridiculed and rejected, I stand in the knowledge that I am divinely connected to my Creator and I identify with Christ Jesus. I realize that I am accepted in the beloved of God. When my father and mother forsake me, the Lord will protect me. I know He will never leave me or forsake me.

9. All things work together for my good because I love God and am called according to His purpose (Romans 8:28). I realize my enemy is not flesh and blood, but evil forces that seek to steal my peace. I am a new creature in Christ Jesus and no weapon formed against me will prosper.

10. I am His workmanship created unto good works. All of my parts, my whole body, in conjunction with my mind, intricately function together in perfect harmony. I am the expression of God's perfect beauty and goodness. I am uniquely made, with a distinct purpose in the earth. No one else is quite like me. I am wonderfully different, yet inextricably connected to the whole of life. The world is better because of my existence.

I am a part of the divine exchange: I inhale and exhale life. I give and I receive. I consume and produce. I am the economy of God.

CHAPTER SEVENTEEN

Guidelines For Deliverance Ministry

Jesus said that Satan is the "father of lies." Jesus is, "the Way, the Truth and the Life." If Jesus, the Truth, says something, we should find ourselves believing Him. He has the *words of life*. Therefore, since Satan is shrewd, perversely intelligent and deceptive, we must depend solely on the Holy Spirit when engaging in the warfare of casting out demons.

The following are **prerequisites** and **strategies** that most deliverance ministers would agree upon:

1. The candidate for deliverance must be aware of what he or she is about to engage in.
2. The candidate must be made aware that deliverance is war and a battle for his or her soul. It is very important for the candidate to express his or her willingness to actively engage in the process of deliverance by cooperating with the deliverance minister as the demons are called out. This may include initiating a cough or exercising authority over the demons. The candidate must not be pas-

sive but forcefully command the spirits to come out also.

3. The candidate must trust you, the minister. You must gain his or her trust by showing compassion.

4. The candidate must be honest and open, realizing that the Holy Spirit will reveal hidden or forgotten things in his or her psyche.

5. The candidate must admit that the spirits are there, otherwise, they will not leave. If one is unable to admit that he or she is under demonic oppression, he or she is inadvertently exercising his or her will to keep them (demons) there.

6. The candidate should understand the concept of *pleading the blood.* Virtually, we as believers have been bought, redeemed, and paid for by the blood of Jesus (1 Corinthians 6: 20). We are owned by God and Satan is a trespasser.

7. The minister and candidate should pray a prayer of submission to the power of the Holy Spirit, binding the demons in and out of the person. Let the person know that he or she has power over the devils and when he or she exercises his or her will by commanding them to go out, they have to go.

Ways God will have ministers bring forth or initiate deliverance

Many times people are not ready to receive deliverance and a wall of resistance has been set up by demonic spirits who do not want the person delivered. It can sometimes cause much difficulty for the minister(s) to initiate deliverance so various strategies can be utilized to get the process started. Of course, these strategies and others must be initiated as the Holy Spirit leads. What is done will depend upon the circumstances of the individual and the stage within the deliverance process. For instance, a hug or a kiss at the right time will bring deliverance to a person who has been starved of love and rejected. When this is done in response to the prompting of the Holy Spirit, His love will cause a person to yield and embrace the love of God. Here are several ways that can help you initiate deliverance. The following are demonstrations of God's love:

1. **A hug** — must be initiated by the Lord. It will always be gentle and will happen after demons have been commanded to come out. Deliverance breaks forth because of the timing and anointing on the hug, coupled with the candidate sensing God's love and compassion at that moment. Sometimes, without any thought of deliverance, people can be set free with a hug by the sovereignty of God.

2. **A gentle touch** — placing the hand where the Holy Spirit directs: on the back, shoulder, neck, stomach; or wherever the Spirit is revealed to be operating.

3. **Kiss on the forehead** — must be initiated by the Holy Spirit. This can happen to confirm a statement of God's love for that person.

4. **Surprise attack** — commanding demons to come out without warning (Acts 16:16).

5. **Using Scripture to affirm Satan's defeat** — Example: Satan you are defeated and you will no longer deceive this person. Jesus defeated you on the cross and in the end; you shall be cast into the lake of fire and brimstone. "You shall be tormented day and night forever and ever" (Revelation 20:10).

6. **Prophesying a personal word from God concerning the person seeking deliverance** — The Word says, "He sent His word to heal them, and delivered them from their destruction" (Ps.107:20). When a prophet or minister speaks a word from God by the Spirit, that word contains the power

and compassion to deliver from depression, confusion, and fear. This will build their self-esteem. The personal word will also help the candidate to understand that God understands their past, is not judging him or her but, accepts him or her and is seeking to set the candidate free.

Another way that God will initiate deliverance is by the minister encouraging the candidate to release a cough. What this means is that there are times when the Holy Spirit is ready to drive the demon out of the person, but the person is passive and not participating in the battle. I will have them participate by opening their mouth and commanding the spirit to come out. There are times when the person is so yielded to God and so strongly desiring deliverance, the demons readily come out. At other times, the person has to be coaxed. I tell him or her to exercise their faith by initiating a cough. I also tell them that one cannot mechanically cough out a spirit. It is done by the power of the Holy Spirit.

However, the individual can cooperate with the Lord by strongly letting the devil know that his time is up with him or her. This can be done by the candidate loudly or forcefully telling the spirit how much he is hated, or loudly commanding it to come out in Jesus' name while simultaneously releasing the cough. After several commands and coughs, the demon knows that the person's will is in agreement with the Lord's will. The Lord also knows it because there is a spiritual yoking in that moment. The power of God explodes and the demons are driven out.

The first time that I experienced this, I was casting devils out of a young girl that had been molested. She had renounced everything that we could remember along with all that God had revealed to us. But nothing happened. I noticed that she looked as if she was choking and kept swallowing. I asked the Holy Spirit what to do and He brought to my mind something that I read in Frank and Ida Mae Hammond's book, *Pigs in the Parlor.* In his book, he shares how sometimes you may have to encourage the candidate to cough a little to get things started.[1] As I thought on this, the Holy Spirit spoke to me and said, "Tell her to cough!" I hesitated, not sure that I should do it, when the Lord spoke again, "Tell her to cough." So I did as I was instructed. As soon as she started coughing, everything broke loose. I was amazed! Devils were coming out of her at every command!

I was thoroughly convinced and since then, I've seen it work multiple times. But let me clarify something. I don't use this technique all of the time. Neither do I depend on it because the Holy Spirit is diverse in His operations. He is the strategizer. One must **always** depend on the Spirit of the living God to strategize and lead us in deliverance warfare.

Dos and Don'ts of Ministry Teams

1. When ministering to a person, do not interrupt someone who is already ministering. Don't think you are the deliverer.
2. Be courteous. Do not try to take over the deliverance ministry. Wait until you are invited. In the meanwhile, pray quietly, and not overbearingly loud.
3. When two are ministering together, remember you are not in competition with each other. While one is ministering, the other should be praying in the Spirit. The Holy Spirit is in charge. He is the strategizer. When one is finished for the moment, look at the other person, you will both sense the Holy Spirit leading the other to flow or minister.
4. Do not allow two or three people at the same time to scream and call out the names of spirits. Demons love confusion. Be patient and pray quietly in the Spirit. If someone feels they have the name

of a spirit, then write it down or whisper it to the lead person. Remember, you are **all** anointed but God isn't going to use you all at once to command them out.

5. Let the person being delivered be in a comfortable position, either sitting, bending over or on their knees.

6. Be patient, loving and attentive to the individual as you're ministering.

7. Be sensitive to each other. The more you minister together as a team the more you understand each other and you will flow together more easily. A yoking together or *oneness* in the Spirit will take place among you.

8. Do not beg demons to leave but command them to come out according to Mark 16:17 and Acts 16:16.

(Mark 16:17) "And these signs will follow those who believe: In My name they will cast out demons..."

(Acts 16:16-18) Now it happened, as we went to prayer, that a certain slave girl possessed with a spirit of divination met us, who brought her masters much profit by fortune-telling. This girl followed Paul and us, and cried out, saying, "These men are the servants of the Most High God, who proclaim to us the way of salvation." And this he did for many days. But Paul, greatly annoyed turned and said to the spirit, "I command you in the name of Jesus Christ to come out of her." And he came out that very hour.

Terminology of warfare words

There are certain words used in spiritual warfare. Some of these words are misunderstood and misused. I hope the following definitions and usage of these terms will help you in effective warfare.

Binding and Loosing

Jesus said in Matthew 18:18, "Whatever you bind on earth is (has been) bound in heaven and whatever you loose on earth is (has been) loosed on the earth." This Scripture has been misused by some who say you can bind a person's mind to Christ by saying I loose your mind from the devil and bind you to Christ." Jesus never taught this. You cannot bind anything to a person's mind. God will not interfere with one's will. He wants a person to freely give himself to Him.

The word *bind* in the Greek is *deo*, which means, *to tie down, or fasten, or put into chains*. The inference is that Satan's ability to function is bound, his hands are tied and his mouth is muffled!

The word *loose* is *luo* in the Greek which means, *to loose anything that is tied up or fastened; to set a captive free who has been imprisoned in the mind or diseased in the body*. Through Matthew 18:18 and Luke 10:17, we have the authority to stop the devil's operation in a person's life by (binding) him and loosing a person from his grip.

How it is done:

"Satan, I bind your work in this person's life. You spirit of alcohol, cursing, and so on. I command you to cease your operation. I loose this person from your grip. Let him go." This can be done in close proximity or at a distance. (See Chapter 7, *Other Ways God Brings Deliverance, Part I — Deliverance through Intercession.*)

Rebuke

In the Greek, the word *rebuke* is epitimao which means, *to censure or admonish as to forbid; to voice a strong disapproval or to condemn as wrong*. So when a Christian rebukes Satan by saying, "I rebuke you Satan in Jesus' name", he is voicing his disapproval of the enemy's work. This is a statement of one's opposition, not an attack on Satan. The word rebuke is a transitive verb and should be followed by a strong directive or command. Jesus is our example.

In Mark 4:35-39, when Jesus and the disciples were crossing the sea, a wind storm arose and frightened the disciples. When Jesus was awakened from sleep, the Word says in verse 39, "Then He arose and rebuked the wind and **said** to the sea, "Peace, be still."

When Jesus revealed His crucifixion to his disciples, Peter rebuked Him. (Mark 8:31-33) In verse 33, He rebuked Peter, saying, "Get behind Me, Satan! For you are not mindful of the things of God, but the things of men."

When the epileptic was brought to Jesus, the Word says that He rebuked the unclean spirit, saying to it: "Deaf and dumb spirit, I command you, come out of him and enter him no more!"

In all three cases, the Lord's rebukes were followed by a strong command: First, "Peace be still"; second, "Get behind me Satan"; and third, "I command you, 'come out of him...'"

In the same way, we as warriors must not stop with the simple, "I rebuke you Satan" but we must follow by commanding him "out and away in Jesus name." In other words, a rebuke is not a rebuke unless a command follows.

Casting down

The words, *casting down* is found in 2 Corinthians 10:5, "Casting down imaginations (arguments) and every high thing that exalts itself against the knowledge of God, bringing every thought into captivity to the obedience of Christ." The Greek word for casting is *kathaireo* which means, "To lower violently; cast, pull, take down or destroy." The above Scripture commands us to throw away, destroy demonic thoughts and images that directly affront our obedience to God's Word, to cast down by commanding the thoughts to go in Jesus' name.

Cast out

The word *cast* is *ekballo*, the Greek word which means, *to eject; drive out or send away*. We believers cast out devils in Jesus' name by commanding them to "come out" in Jesus' name!", "Go", "Leave, in Jesus' name," "Up and out, in Jesus' name!"

Pleading the blood of Jesus does not cast devils out. Pleading the blood of Jesus by repeatedly saying, "I plead the blood of Jesus", does not cast the devil out. Pleading the blood is literally telling Satan what the blood of Jesus has done for the candidate being delivered. The blood has redeemed him (Colossians 1:14), delivered him and purchased him (Acts 20:28), and so on.

What this does is agitate and confuse the devil, causing the demons to weaken and loose their hold on the person. This must be followed by commanding the demons out of the person.

Unauthorized warfare vs. authorized warfare

Never attempt to go to war where God has not sent you. When one goes into Satan's territory unauthorized there is no protection. Wherever the Lord sends you, He will not only equip you to do the work, but He gives you the authority and power over demons in that person or territory. This is called your *realm of rule*. The phrase realm of rule is a term used to describe a particular area of authority that a person may possess in order to govern his assigned arena of ministry. This power is delegated by a higher authority and this higher authority assigns all the powers it possesses to its representative, including all military might to battle any opposing forces. This higher authority is God.

He sends an entourage of mighty angels to protect you and do warfare around you and in the heavenlies. Though we possess this divine power and protection, it is only good in our own sphere of ministry. We cannot assume that we can go into another man's area of rule and be productive. We can only be effective in our assigned duties. God's power and presence will only go with us where He has sent us.

The biblical example is found in Acts 19, where we find the apostle Paul doing the work of an evangelist, preaching the Word, ministering the Holy Spirit, performing miracles, and exercising power over demons by the anointing that was upon him.

"Now, God worked unusual miracles by the hands of Paul. So that even handkerchiefs or aprons were brought from his body to the sick, and the diseases left them and the evil spirits went out of them" (Acts 19:11, 12). This Scripture demonstrates the authority God had given Paul in Ephesus.

His realm of authority is further demonstrated in verses 13 and 14 of the same chapter: "Then some of the itinerant Jewish exorcists took it upon themselves to call the name of the Lord Jesus over those who had evil spirits, saying, 'We exorcise you by the Jesus whom Paul preaches.' Also, there were seven sons of Sceva, a Jewish chief priest who did so. And the evil spirit answered and said, 'Jesus I know, and Paul I know, but who are you?' Then the man in whom the evil spirit was, leaped on them, overpowered them, and prevailed against them, so that they fled out of that house naked and wounded." These *vagabond* Jews had no authority because they were not born again, not Spirit filled, nor commissioned or sent by God, and therefore had no power in that territory.

The following are true examples of what can happen when we go into Satan's territory unauthorized:

Woman with a legion – Unauthorized warfare
My friend Angela, was deceived by Satan to visit the mental institution and pray for her brother, although she had not been saved very long and possessed a limited understanding of deliverance. He had been mentally dis-

turbed since he was nineteen years of age and had been hospitalized for about twenty years. The enemy deceived her by telling her to "go to the hospital and pray for your brother. You have power to heal him." Believing she had the power, she obeyed the *voice*. She went to the hospital without anyone knowing her intentions. But because she was not sent by God and not prepared, she opened herself up to an invasion of hundreds of demons. The atmosphere in a mental hospital is full of demonic activity. Demons fill the air. Because she was in their territory unprotected, the demons entered her mouth as she tried to cast them out.

She later called me because her tongues had changed. As I listened to her, I realized her tongues had indeed become demonic. Later that night, we sat her down and began casting spirits out of her. Witchcraft was the first to go. Then, self-deception, fear, fantasy, rebellion, and so forth. That was only the beginning of her deliverance.

A couple of days later, I went to her house and by the word of knowledge, God revealed things from her past such as, rejection, hurts, anger, bitterness, and so forth. This went on for hours until I finally asked the Lord how many demons had entered her. He replied, "Legion" (Mark 5:9). The demon told Jesus its name was *legion*, referencing a Roman military unit of about six thousand soldiers. Regardless of the number, Angela had multiple evil spirits which needed to be expelled. Some of the spirits had entered her during the years prior to this incident. But when she went to the hospital unassigned, many, many more entered her.

The process of deliverance took about three weeks. After several days of casting many demons out of her, God sovereignly continued the process. She would foam at the mouth all night as demons continued leaving her. At the end of the three-week period, the legion left her, leaving just one. It was a spirit of death that tormented her day and night threatening to kill her. He told her continually, "Bow down and worship me or I'm going to kill you." This brought great fear to her. Finally, in desperation, this sister cried out to the Lord saying, "I don't want to worship the devil. Lord, you kill me! Don't let him kill me! You kill me!" Then, she threw herself on the bed and cried herself to sleep.

When Angela woke up the next morning, the tormenting spirit was gone. She arose, took a shower and dressed herself. She went out to eat breakfast which was something she had not done in three weeks. Her mother saw the great change and began to cry and praise the Lord. She has been free ever since and is now used mightily in healing and deliverance.

Personal testimony #1 – Unauthorized warfare

Some years ago, in the beginning of my ministry, I was asked by a friend to come and cast devils out of her husband. Her name was Jean. At that time, we were all members of the same church. Initially, her husband Carl and her entire family had been very active in the church. Then, I started to notice that Carl stopped talking to people and later started sitting in the back of the church. This continued until he eventually stopped coming to church altogether.

One day his wife told me that he had succumbed to spirits of pornography. He stopped taking baths and wouldn't leave his room anymore. She asked me to come to her home to see if I could help him. I told her I would. But as time went by, he grew worse. Finally, because she was so distraught, I decided to drop everything and go to her home. She told me she thought it was too late. It would probably be better if I waited because he was so despondent he probably wouldn't be receptive. I had the feeling that she was right but because I felt that I could really help him and wanted to see him free, I made up my mind to go anyway.

When I arrived at her house, Jean persistently informed me that he wasn't ready. But I insisted she call him downstairs. Reluctantly Carl came down. I asked if I could pray for him. All three of us joined hands, but before we prayed, I saw a demon come down behind Carl, jab him in the back with his horns and literally pull him two or three steps backwards. Before I could respond, another dark spirit came down the steps, circled us, came behind me and attacked my neck. I tried to pray, but with very little confidence or power. I knew in that moment, it was fruitless to try anymore because there was no anointing. By this time, I was **more** than willing to agree with Jean that he was not ready. We agreed to try again some other time, but I knew in my heart he was beyond my ability to help him.

After I left her home I realized that I had been attacked by an evil spirit because my neck began to hurt. I tried to ignore the pain, thinking it would pass, but it persisted and lasted about a week. That day, I learned a painful lesson that we believers are never to assume we can go and cast devils out of someone against **their** will. Neither can we minister in any power or anointing if God has not approved of it or **sent** us.

Personal Testimony #2 – Authorized warfare

While in Kitali, Kenya, I experienced the power and anointing that can rest upon a believer when he or she is sent to a region to minister.

Before I left for Kenya, I prayed and asked God whether or not He was sending me to that country, because I was not going anywhere without His anointing. The Lord assured me that it was His will for me to go. There was no reason for me to worry because His angels would be with me to protect me.

Upon arriving in Kitali, while others in our group stayed in rooms on the church compound, I was assigned to a room in a local hotel. About three o'clock in the morning, I had a visitor. In between sleep and wake I heard a hissing sound and realized that a serpent was trying to strike me. I was sleeping under a mosquito net and could feel the net brushing up against my back every time I felt this thing striking at me. I struggled to wake up and when I finally did, I jumped out of bed, grabbed the knife, a flashlight from the dresser and began looking under the bed to find the snake. All the while I was looking; the Lord whispered to me that this encounter was spiritual, not natural. Still, I kept looking until finally, I was satisfied that there was nothing in the room. Yet, I was frustrated because here I was in a foreign country, at this moment, by myself, having experienced this very real encounter with a snake and no explanation.

I sat in a chair and began to pray in the Spirit (tongues). Again, the Lord reminded me that this was spiritual and that there was no natural snake in the room. As I continued to pray in the Spirit, my spiritual eyes opened and I saw a huge black snake across the room staring at me. I was not afraid because I was in the Spirit where there is no fear.

The Lord informed me that I was to start laughing because he was going to teach me a new form of warfare. In obedience to God, I began to laugh naturally, in my own strength. In a few moments the Holy Spirit engaged Himself and the laughter became supernatural. I had never experienced this type of laughter. It was coming out of me in different forms and cadences, sometimes slow, steady, rhythmic laughter, and then very rapid like machine gun fire. The Lord again opened my eyes and I saw the snake. Only this time he was holding his hands up, turning from side to side, trying to protect his face! The laughter coming out of my mouth were flashes of supernatural light striking the evil spirit in the head, driving it backwards! The Lord told me to keep laughing because it was a supernatural weapon and the demon would have to leave. A few moments later the Holy Spirit informed me that the thing had left.

Afterwards, the Lord opened my ears so I could hear what was going on in the Spirit. He allowed me to hear this snake having a conversation with a principality somewhere in the spirit realm. I heard the higher ranking demon ask, "What happened, were you effective?" The snake replied, "No. I went to his room to frighten him, but it didn't work. I was driven away. He has **authority** here because the Holy One sent him."

Because of this encounter with evil and the victory the Holy Spirit brought through His weapon of holy laughter, I found the confidence to minister throughout the two weeks I spent in Kenya. The Lord also taught me the awesome power available to believers when we are **sent by God**. No matter where we go in this world, if we are **sent by Him,** no demon in hell can stand against us. Hallelujah!

[1]Frank Hammond and Ida Mae Hammond, <u>Pigs In The Parlor</u> (Kirkwood, Missouri: Impact Books, 1973), page 59

APPENDIX

Common Questions Concerning Deliverance

The following are common questions that I've heard people ask over the years throughout my ministry. I hope that my answers will help bring better understanding to you:

1. Where do demons go when they are expelled?

I have heard others tell demons to "Go into the abyss", "Go to the city dump" or even, "Go to hell". But do we have the power to cast them into any places other than where Jesus sent them? Jesus never told them to go anywhere except, "Come out!"

As a matter of fact, in the account of the mad man of Gaderenes, the demon begged Jesus not to torment him. "And he cried out with a loud voice and said, 'What have I to do with You, Jesus, Son of the Most High God? I implore You by God that You do not torment me'" (Mark 5:7).

Then, in Luke 8:31, the same demons begged Him not to send them to the "abyss." Again, the same situation is found in Matthew 8:29 where demons spoke of the time

215

and place of their demise. "And suddenly they cried out, saying, "What have we to do with You, Jesus, You Son of God? Have You come here to torment us before the time?" This is an indication that there is a set time for Satan and demons to be judged and cast into the abyss, the bottomless pit (Revelation 9:1,11).

Apparently, the Lord Jesus understood this because He complied with their request and cast them into the swine.

So where do they go when they are cast out? Jesus said in Matthew 12:43 that "When the unclean spirit goes out of a man, he goes through dry places, seeking rest, and finds none."

Apparently, "dry places" is a restless place on the earth where there is no access to human beings. For a moment, they are cut off from working their evil through a human being. (Job 30:3-8) I believe they automatically go to this dry place. But many times, I help them along by **commanding** them to go there.

2. Can a person cast demons out of someone while needing deliverance himself?

A minister can cast devils out of a person even though he may need some deliverance himself.

Casting devils out is an act of faith and obedience to God's command to "...cast out devils..." (Matthew 10:8). It is not by the might or holiness of man that demons are expelled, but by the power of the Holy Spirit in us.

Deliverance is a process, and even though we may have rid ourselves of certain demonic strongholds or oppressions, there is always room for more purging. Sometimes as a minister, while casting demons out of a person, we may go through deliverance ourselves.

Every deliverance minister should submit him or herself to a purging ever so often. It is a known fact that if there are certain kindred spirits in both the minister and the candidate, it can hinder the effectiveness of the deliverance session.

For instance, once while casting a spirit of death out of a young man, another young man named Colin tried to help us but he had not yet been purged. As soon as he said, "Come out" a demon of death manifested in Colin and we had to cast demons out of him also.

Note: Colin had been using drugs and had not repented nor was delivered. Consequently, he was ineffective in warfare. Before attempting to cast demons out of anyone, make sure there is **no sin** in your life. Demons are cast out by faith and confidence in your relationship with God. If there is sin and there is no faith, you will not be effective.

3. Is it necessary to yell loudly when casting out demons?

Yelling at demons **does not** affect them one way or another. Yelling loudly doesn't give you any more power or authority. Demons only respond to the supernatural power of the Holy Ghost. The Greater One indwells us (1 John 4:4) and it is by **His** power that demons are expelled. Mark 16:17 says, "In My name (Jesus) shall they cast out devils." It is in His name, by the power of the Holy Spirit, through our faith that demons flee. It is not how loudly you speak, but by your firmness and authority that they obey.

The Lord once gave me a dream concerning this matter. In the dream I was casting out devils and I was yelling real loud. The Lord spoke these words to me, "Son, you don't have to yell at them, just **command** them to come out!"

Since then, I've not only learned that it's not necessary to yell, but you can command them to come out in a whisper and they will go. It is all in knowing who you are and the power you possess in Christ. (See chapter 5, *Authority of the Believer*.)

4. Should children be present when deliverances take place?

There are times when deliverance will break out without any warning. God sovereignly moves and there is no time to remove any children who are present.

In the *School of Prayer and Healing*, while teaching or ministering prophetically, the Lord will inspire me to call out a demonic sickness or oppression (fear, bitterness, arthritis, etc.) and corporate deliverance will take place. Many times when this happens, there are children present. To my knowledge, no child has ever been attacked. As a matter of fact at times we have had children participate in casting out demons.

But, in general, it should be understood that parents should counsel their children in warfare. They should be taught what is going on so they won't be afraid. Children are very flexible and intelligent. They take their cues from their parents. If parents show strength and fortitude, the children will do likewise.

However, as a rule, all children, no matter the age, should be protected — especially those that are very young. They should be covered by the Blood of Jesus with angels stationed about them.

The following is a model prayer to cover children at any time:

"Father, let the protective blood of Jesus cover this child (these children). I bind any spirits and I forbid any attack against them according to Isaiah 54:17 which says, '"No weapon formed against *them* shall prosper, and every tongue which rises against *them* in judgment *we* shall condemn. This is the heritage of the servants of the Lord, and their righteousness is from Me, says the Lord"'. May the angels of the Lord stand guard over my child (children) according to Psalms 91:10-11, "'No evil shall befall *us*, Nor shall any plague come near *our* dwelling; For He shall give His angels charge over them, to keep them in all *their* ways."'(italics added) I commit _____into your hands, in Jesus' name, Amen."

There are times when the whole family is involved in a deliverance session, but when the children are not involved, I send them out to another room. Sometimes "grown-ups" deliverances are not for the children to see. Moreover, be led of the Spirit.

5. Is it necessary to know the name of every demon in order to cast them out?

No. But since demons are legalistic, there are times when they will hide behind a name. For example, if you are commanding a spirit of fornication to come out, he may resist because his job is to cause a person to rape someone. Other spirits may be from the perversion group. One may be a spirit of sodomy, while another may be called a demon of oral sex. The Holy Spirit will reveal to you who they are.

If you don't know their names, but know their work; call them out by what they do. For example, you may say, "Demon that causes this woman to have difficulty breathing, come out in Jesus' name" or "Demon that causes headaches, come out."

They will respond:

6. Can you cast demons out of anyone including a sinner?

No. It would make no sense to cast a demon out of a sinner unless he is about to be saved just as in Acts 8:6-8, "And the multitudes with one accord heeded the things spoken by Philip, hearing and seeing the miracles which he did. For unclean spirits, crying with a loud voice, came out of many who were possessed; and many who were paralyzed and lame were healed. And there was great joy in that city."

According to Matthew 12:44-45, demonic spirits will only reenter a person because his body is not filled with God. He doesn't belong to God, therefore there is no protection from an unclean spirit who has legal authority to reenter someone who opens up himself to sin again, like in this Scripture: "Then he (the demon) says, 'I will return to my house from which I came.' And when he comes, he finds it empty, swept, and put in order. Then he goes and takes with him seven other spirits more wicked than himself, and they enter and dwell there; and the last state of that man is worse than the first. So shall it also be with this wicked generation."

When God cleanses a person, it is for the purpose of serving Him. Even though a person may be a Christian, if he refuses to surrender his life to God, he cannot be delivered. As much as we may desire to see a brother or sister delivered, there is nothing we can do if they embrace their sin and continue to walk in rebellion.

7. How do we bring a person to a place of deliverance?

The purpose of deliverance is to bring a person into a greater intimate relationship with Jesus. So if that person (your son, friend, husband, etc.) is saved, but not living for the Lord, one must enter into intercessory warfare on their behalf. I believe this type of intercession would include praying in the Spirit (Romans 8:26) and praying with our understanding.

When we pray in tongues, we are praying the perfect prayer for someone. We are discovering demonic operations in their lives and restoring their relationship with God by binding and loosing in the Spirit. Demons are exposed and God secretly does a work in that person's life to bring them to a greater revelation of Christ.

As we pray the Word (Ephesians 1:16-18 and Ephesians 3:16-19), we give the Holy Spirit freedom to minister Christ's love, wisdom and understanding to our loved one. With greater revelation of Him and by experiencing more of His love, they will be drawn to Him and His delivering power.

According to Matthew 18:18, we have the power to bind up hindering spirits and pray God's salvation and deliverance into the life of the saved or unsaved. For it is not God's will that anyone should perish, but that all would come unto repentance.

8. Is it necessary to open windows and doors when casting demons out of a person or their home?

Demons like angels are supernatural beings. They are not bound by earthly matter (earth, wind, and fire). They can walk through trees, homes, walls, etc. They can live in your furnace, air ducts, chimney, sewer, etc. It really doesn't matter.

When you cast them out, they fly right through the walls into dry places. Protect your home by following the steps found in Chapter Four, *Determining the Need for Deliverance* and in the section, *Steps to Maintain One's Deliverance.*

About The Author

Prophet Lee Williams is an apostolic prophet with a compassionate heart for the nations. He has spent the last two decades teaching and preaching with the demonstration of the prophetic anointing in his life. God called Lee to raise up and equip prophets in the Body of Christ, and to simultaneously develop prophetic healing and deliverance teams that will minister evangelistically, in every segment of life.

Lee Williams is founder and president of *Merciful Ministries of Jesus Christ,* a ministry founded upon Hebrews 4:16, *Let us therefore come boldly unto the throne of grace, that we may obtain mercy and find grace to help in time of need.* The heart of *Merciful Ministries* focuses on healing the brokenhearted, setting the captives free and restoring the Body of Christ to reach the harvest locally, nationally and internationally.

He presides over the *Merciful Ministries School of Prayer and Healing,* in which the Holy Spirit moves mightily in deliverance, signs, wonders, and miracles. He is also the director of the *Lee Williams Apostolic and Prophetic Training School,* where people from all walks of life are being trained to go to the nations.

Notes:

Notes: